MW01269201

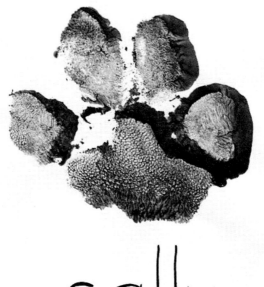

sally

Life With Sally

Princess Tails

Tricia L. McDonald

Life With Sally

Published 2017
Printed in the United States of America
ISBN 978-1-939294-47-0

Cover design by Jacob Kubon

Cover photo and title page cover by Nick Tremmel

Published by

splatteredinkpress.com

To my little princess.

Table of Contents

Eli's New Game

Eli, our jack Russell/Australian cattle dog, is a rescue dog who came with his own idiosyncrasies that have nothing to do with Sally. He is terrified of thunder and the sound of gun shots. When I say terrified, I mean flying-onto-your-lap and trying-to-burrow-through-you terrified. He also has this licking thing where he will lick and lick and lick without stopping until you make him stop. Oh, and there is his fetish with linens that sort of goes along with the licking thing. He licks sheets, pillowcases and blankets until they just about disintegrate and then he eats them. We went through many pillowcases and sheets when we first got him; and found a plethora of linen pieces while poop-scooping.

But lately Eli has developed a couple of new peculiarities. My smart phone dinged when someone sent me a message the other day. Eli's head shot up, his eyes got crazy, and like a flash he was up and running. In a leap he landed on my lap and started pawing at me. At first I had no idea what brought on the sudden frenzy, but after similar happenings over the next couple of days, I made the connection between the dings and his craziness. I wasn't sure how to handle this new situation. For the fear of thunder noise, we always give Eli meds. We have to give them to him about three hours ahead of time in order for them to work effectively. If we took the same approach with the phone or computer dings, he would be walking around in a constant state of drugged. We don't want that.

I explained the situation to Mike and his suggestion was that I change the ding to another sound. *That's ridiculous*, I thought. I stopped at our vet's office to pick up some medications and explained the new Eli situation.

"I'm not sure what to do," I said. Dr. Jackson looked a bit perplexed as we talked for a few minutes.

"Maybe try changing it to another sound?" she said. I hate it when Mike is right.

That afternoon I re-programmed the noises in my phone and computer. I thought I found some good replacements, but it is an ongoing process every time there is a new noise and I see Eli's reaction.

Now he has a new phenomenon that happens in the middle of the night. The dogs sleep in our bedroom with us and we keep the bedroom door closed at night to keep them from wandering (and Eli from peeing) in other parts of the house. Sally sleeps in bed with us and Eli sleeps on the fluffy pillow in his kennel or on the recliner. We tried letting him sleep with us, but there is that whole linen fetish and licking thing. Plus, he doesn't like to jump up on the bed.

One night, I woke to Eli standing alongside the bed, scratching at the mattress in an obvious attempt to get my attention.

"What's up buddy? Do you need to go outside?" I slurred as I stumbled to the front door with him following close at my heels.

"Go take care of business," I said as I opened the door to the cold night air. He looked outside, up at me and then sprinted back to the bedroom and into his kennel. I got back in bed, snuggled into the blankets and fell back to sleep. Within minutes, Eli was back at the side of the bed again. I reached over and petted his head, listening for any noises that might be frightening him, and couldn't hear any.

I got up so I could lift him onto the bed thinking he wanted to be near us. As I got out, Eli ran into this kennel.

"Come on, Eli," I whispered. He stayed in his kennel so I got back in bed and curled around

Sally, who was snoring through this whole ordeal. Just like Mike.

I started dozing again when Eli returned. I got up, reached for him and he ran into this kennel. Back into my bed I climbed and once again, after I was snuggled in, he returned to pawing at the side of the mattress. I'm not very happy at this point, but I get out again and yes, he ran into his kennel.

"I'm done playing, Eli," I said as I shut and locked the kennel door. He waited until I was back in bed and then he started whimpering. Pretty soon he was whining and kept getting louder. I got up, opened his kennel door, and as he bounded out, I picked him up and put him in bed with us.

Needless to say, that's when the licking started.

A Sally Model

"Tricia, don't do that to her," Mike says.

"Do what?" I ask in fake confusion.

We are standing in Must Love Dogs, a doggy boutique in downtown Grand Haven, where I am debuting the newest Life With Sally book, <u>Waggin' More Tails.</u> I am holding Sally who is wearing a knitted hat. It is a great hat that covers her ears and I've had my eye on it since we came in.

The truth of the matter is that this is a perfect opportunity to give the Sally-Diva a chance to model a number of different, fun clothing items.

We snap a few photos of Sally wearing the knitted hat and I put her down while I look around for another fun thing to put on her.

Tonya, the owner of Must Love Dogs, comes over with a 2-inch wide black diamond studded collar.

"Let's try this," she says.

Sally starts to walk away, but I call her and she comes back—although I notice she is not wagging her tail in celebration. She gives me that "really, mom?" look, but I ignore it and put the collar around her neck. She gives a long shake, but it stays on.

"Hmmm, doesn't really work," I say and Tonya agrees. We snap a few photos anyway. I mean, why humiliate Sally if we aren't going to have some pictures to show for it?

I spot a red fur piece with long brown reindeer antlers, a black faux belt and an attached hat hanging on the wall behind our table of books.

"Yes!" I say. Scooting alongside the table, I reach as far as possible but still can't get to it. I lean a little farther, the table scrapes against the floor, and Sally darts to the other side of the room. I'm not sure if she just spotted the object of my desire or if the noise startled her. It doesn't really matter because I am able to grab it off the hanger.

"Come here, Sal," I say. She starts walking away from me and toward Mike, but I head her off and put the outfit on her. The bells on the door tinkle and several women walk in. Sally wags her tail and walks toward them. I think she is looking for attention or an escape through the open door.

"She's so cute," one of the women says.

I have my camera again and start snapping photos of the Sally–Deer, begging her to look at me, to which she grudgingly obliges. We leave it on for a few minutes as I talk about the book— after all, that is the real reason we are here.

I take the outfit off Sally and start looking around for the next clothing apparel to put on the little white dog, when the door opens again. It's Hannah Bruce, one of our favorite Sally fans.

"Hi Hannah," I say. Sally walks over to see her as well. "You just have to see Sally in this great hat."

I grab the knitted hat again and put it over Sally's head. "How cute is this?" I ask.

Hannah shakes her head a little and gives Sally, what I think is an apologetic pat.

"No?" I ask. I don't really wait for an answer as Hannah and I head toward the table. Her dad, Jesse, asks if she would like the new book, to which Hannah gives him the best "duh" look I have ever seen and I get to work signing it for her. Before they leave the store, I get a big hug and Jesse takes a photo of Sally, Hannah and me together.

After they leave, Mike comes over and removes the hat from Sally's head and walks away with it. I think his plan is to hide it from me, but that's okay because I just spotted the cutest faux leopard dress that will look adorable on her.

Snowing...Again

"It snowed again," I say to Mike as I pull the curtains open. I crawl back into bed, pulling the comforter up to my chin. Outside the ground is blanketed with several new inches of blindingly white snow. This is on top of the two or three feet already covering the ground.

"Shocking," Mike says, sarcasm dripping.

It has been snowing for months here in Michigan and since it is only January we know there are months of winter left. That means more snow. We are feeling housebound, not only by the snow but also the frigid cold that has settled into our little world. My attention is distracted by Sally and Eli, chasing each other into the bedroom.

"They seem a little antsy too," I say. Eli finds a stream of sunlight and lays down, stretching in the ray.

"Let's take them for a walk," Mike says.

I shiver, just thinking about going outside, but the lure of sunshine drags me out from under the covers.

Thirty minutes later, after feeding the dogs and pulling on layers of clothes, we head out. The single digit air freezes the hairs in my nose, and I pull up my scarf. I have a momentary desire to turn around and head back into the house, but I resist and trudge after Mike and the dogs.

Mike has his snowshoes strapped on, but since I don't own a pair yet, I am wearing my knee-high snow boots. We walk down the plowed driveway with Mike leading the way, Eli behind him, Sally following Eli, and me bringing up the rear. Half-way down, Mike turns right, climbs over the snow bank and starts creating a path in the three feet of snow in the yard. Eli makes the leap and continues following him.

Sally is wearing her purple coat and knitted hat that covers her ears. She stops behind Eli and looks at me.

"It's okay Sal," I say. "I'm coming." With that, she jumps onto the bank, her paws kicking up funnels of snowflakes.

The snow is glistening and so white in the bright sunshine it is almost blinding. The dogs' tracks are the only marks in this beautiful white winter wonderland and I smile, despite the cold. I am invigorated by the beauty around me, and I follow them into the snow bank and sink knee deep. My next step stays on top of the snow, but with the next I sink up to my thigh. This is no longer fun.

"Hey," my voice breaks the silence. Mike stops and turns his head my way. Both of my legs are now stuck deep in the snow. "I'm not too sure about this." The dogs turn and look at me.

"Go on back," Mike says. "I'll just walk around the lake a couple times and create a path." He continues and Eli follows close behind.

I'm determined to make it around the lake at least once, thinking about the calories I'll burn and then the huge breakfast I can have once we're done. I pull my leg out of the snow and move forward, albeit at a very slow pace.

Sally has now walked back and circled around so she is following behind me. I develop a jerky momentum and after a few yards, I stop to catch my breath and check on Sally. What I see when I turn around is her tail as she makes her way back to driveway. She is no longer able to stay on top of the snow as she sinks into the holes created by my footsteps.

"Where ya going, Sal?" She stops and looks back at me, then continues toward the plowed driveway. I consider following her, but I move forward instead, stopping often to catch my breath as each footstep results in sinking deep into the snow.

Twelve hours later—okay I admit that is a huge exaggeration—I finish my trek around the lake and am back on the driveway. I lean over, put my hands on my knees and try to get my breathing under control. My legs tremble as I start walking toward the house, away from Mike and Eli who are making their second trip around.

Big fluffy flakes fall from the sky turning the world into a giant snowglobe and I am trying to see the beauty in it, but at that moment I am sick of the white crap. I want to see green grass, buds on trees and even asphalt. With my head down, I continue my walk, grousing about the weather under my breath and then I hear a familiar bark. *Sally?* I look up and standing on the porch with her tail wagging her whole body is my little white dog. Her silly hat has slipped a bit on her head giving her a goofy look, and as she starts her happy spin, kicking up the snow around her, I can't help but smile and even appreciate the beauty of nature surrounding me.

I'm still counting the days until spring, though.

Snowing...Again

Sally Weirdness Continues

"I have to write a new Sally story for the magazine and I'm really struggling," I say to Mike.

"Running out of things to write about?" he asks.

"She just isn't being weird enough. Or rather, she's weird but she isn't giving me any new weird."

Mike raises an eyebrow.

I have been writing a monthly column about Sally for almost seven years now. That is over 84 articles—84 times Sally has provided me with something to write about. When I started the column, I created experiences like a pet psychic who came over and explained why Sally didn't like our cat, Louis. Turns out, Louis was a bit conceited.

Once I took Sally for a doggy massage at Must Love Dogs. She was a bit wiggly which made the massage more interesting.

I started running out of things to create so I started writing about everyday things Sally did. Turns out, she is a bit on the odd side and her readers love her for that.

She found a garden rake and decided she was going to own it—seriously! She dragged that rake everywhere and became a bit psychotic about it, until her doggy dentist said, "No more rake for Sally," after he discovered a hole in her gums. Even her first appointment (and follow-up appointments) with Dr. Moore (her doggy dentist) have been fodder for columns.

There was the time I thought I saw magic in her eyes when she was watching the butterflies flitting around the butterfly bushes. She would sit still in the middle of the bush with the butterflies flying around her head. I was beyond excited when I snapped the photos, right up until that moment when Sally opened her mouth and snatched a butterfly right out of the air.

But my favorite Sally experience has to be knowing a dog that actually licks toads. I mean, why? I couldn't even count the number of toads I have saved from the sloppy tongue of a little white dog. Picking them up—covered in doggy spit—and relocating them to the fenced-in garden just so Sally will leave them alone. One early rainy evening I couldn't get Sally to come in out of the rain because the edges of the pond were teaming with toads laying eggs. She was making herself crazy following one, then another and then another.

Speaking of the pond, we called her the piped piper of fish when she would wander around the edges and the bass followed her. At one time we counted eleven of them following her as she meandered around looking for toads.

She has had numerous visits with Santa— none of them were what I would call a success, but have been interesting. I have dragged her to many classrooms where she has put up with hundreds of children loving on her. We have attended book signings together and events like the PetExpo where fans lined up to see her.

I've written about the fruit she loves to eat and how she picks the strawberries, raspberries, and blueberries herself. And I can't forget the not-so-fun experience of rushing her to the vet after she ate a dead, decaying squirrel.

Every column has also included a photo which often proved interesting as Miss Sally is not always cooperative when it comes to getting her picture taken. In fact, Sally and I even turned getting a photo of her into a column.

I think I may have even written another column about the frustration of running out of things to write about. Sally is nine years old now so I have been writing about her for most of her life. I hate to think that she is getting boring as she gets older, but maybe ...

"She's not weird anymore, eh?" Mike says as he looks at Sally. I follow his gaze and see her sitting statuesque in front of the fireplace, staring into the fire. When I move, I see that she is actually staring at her reflection in the glass in front of the fireplace.

"Well, maybe there is hope for more weirdness," I say.

The Photo Shoot

As I was putting the <u>Life With Sally: Waggin' More Tails</u> book together, I realized it had been quite a while since I had any updated author photos taken. I am always taking photos of Sally, but don't often take any of myself. Since I had met a photographer earlier in the year and loved his work, I called Nick Tremmel.

Nick and I decided that outdoor scenes would be fun since I wanted to get photos of Sally and me together, also. We set a date for a few months down the road when we thought the weather would be nicer.

When the day came I fretted over what to wear, and then decided to go with an outfit that was super comfortable so I wouldn't be focusing on my attire. Of course I pulled out Sally's bling collar and fastened it around her neck. She was stunning!

Nick arrived and we started by taking some photos in my office. Sally ran around like a maniac, spinning and knocking stuff over, but I couldn't get mad at her because she was happy. Plus, I wanted her to stay that way for her photo shoot. Nick took shots of me from different angles, and I tried to smile 'normally,' for whatever that was worth.

"Just try to relax," Nick said. "I promise we'll get pictures that you like." He was so calming and nice to work with that I started to loosen up. At one point he even stood on a chair and took photos of me looking up at him. Totally natural, of course.

After a bit, we headed outside with the little white whirling dervish. Outside she was even happier—if that was possible. Nick suggested I get Sally to do some stuff. Stuff? Like what? Sally doesn't do stuff, especially when I want her to. I did have my pockets full of treats though, and that was a good start.

Nick stretched out on the grass and it was my job to stand behind him and call Sally so he could get snapshots at her level. This didn't work too well because she wouldn't come right up to him, instead she went around him. So I called her to come toward us, and then told her to sit. Yeah, right. Since she knew I had treats, she wasn't going to sit unless it was right by me. I tried throwing the treats near Nick, but I wasn't a good shot and most of them bounced off him. That scared Sally so she really stayed away from him.

"Who controls who here?" Nick asked at one point. Did he really have to ask?

We decided to walk around the pond with Sally, but when she ran ahead of us I realized that photos from that perspective would only present her rear end. Those were not the photos I was envisioning.

"Why don't you walk toward me down this path?" Nick said. I turned, started walking and called the princess.

"Look up at me as you walk," Nick said. "Don't worry about what Sally is doing." He didn't realize that I look down when I walk outside to avoid stepping in something undesirable left by the dogs. We did this several times with Sally and me walking back and forth. Then her majesty got bored and headed down to the pond to look for frogs and such.

We went to the picnic table and I sat Sally on top of it so we were at face level with each other. With her muscles taut and her eyes bugging, we decided terrified would not be a good look for photos.

After a couple hours we decided we had enough photos to choose from and I suggested Nick put his camera down so I could take snapshots of the photographer with Sally. You know, in case I decided to write a story about the event. Of course that was when Sally ran right up to Nick, rolled over for tummy rubs and he provided her with plenty. Without his camera in hand, he was her best buddy.

I was a little nervous about how the photos were going to turn out, but couldn't have been happier. And my favorite is Sally and me walking down the path as I look down at her and she looks up at me. Just me and my little Sal.

(Photo by blinkPHOTO - thinkblinkphoto.com)

The Photo Shoot

Frog Legs

After weeding and working in the yard, I headed off for a stroll around our one acre pond. It only took a few minutes before Sally noticed and became my sidekick.

She took off ahead of me and ran to the pile of corn we kept well-stocked for the ducks in the neighborhood. The day before I had heard a loud wailing and when I looked up from picking strawberries, I had seen Eli chasing something through the woods. That something turned out to be a baby deer, not much bigger than Eli.

"Eli!" I said as I dropped my bowl of strawberries and sprinted toward him. He didn't even hesitate as he continued chasing the poor little screaming baby. I ran tripping over branches and trying to stay upright, as my feet became tangled in vines and thorns grabbed at my socks.

Soon the two of them were out of sight and I ran for back-up.

"Mike," I said, trying to catch my breath. "Eli's chasing a fawn."

Mike jumped on his tractor and took off, while I rubbed at the scratches on my legs and limped in the same direction. Within minutes, Eli had come out of the woods panting. I checked him for blood 1) to make sure he hadn't caught the little fawn and hurt it; and, 2) to make sure the fawn hadn't led Eli to the momma who then hurt Eli. He looked okay, albeit a little exhausted.

And where was Sally during this whole episode? Searching for toads in the strawberry patch and eating the strawberries that had fallen out of the bowl I dropped.

Now on our walk, Sally was searching the area for deer poop in the diminishing corn pile. Our backyard was a poop smorgasbord for Eli and Sally. Between the deer, squirrels, ducks and whatever else visited in the cloak of darkness, there was a plethora of poop.

As I walked along, I saw a beautiful huge bullfrog sitting along the edge of the pond. I love frogs so I was ecstatic! I snuck closer to get a good look when the little white dog lumbered within inches of it. Two things happened at that moment. First, the frog didn't move and second, Sally didn't even see him. Then the princess walked back the way she had come and again, she didn't see the frog and it didn't move. I was stunned and took the time to run to the house and grab my camera. When I got back, the frog was in the same exact spot.

Now I was curious. Why would this frog be sitting in one spot for so long, especially with the little white dog and me coming so close? I thought maybe it was a female laying eggs, but I didn't see any frog eggs in the water near her so that idea was out. It didn't seem injured, so I was stumped but happy, because it gave me the opportunity to take great photos.

Sally's entourage of bass were gathering in the pond nearby and I spotted three or four of them following her as she continued to meander back and forth. After a bit, she spotted the frog and gave it a nudge with her long white snout. It jumped farther onto land, which surprised the heck out of me. *Why didn't it jump into the water away from us?* Sally nosed it again and this time it almost jumped on top of me. Now I was really confused and even Sally looked perplexed. Eli seemed curious as he took a sniff at the frog that had nowhere left to go except into the pond. When he landed in the water, there was a lot of splashing as the three bass lunged at him. It took about a second for him to leap back onto the bank. Now I understood why he was staying out of the water.

"Mike," I yelled across the pond. "We might have to thin the bass herd."

He looked over and gave me a nod that meant he couldn't hear me, and then went back to weeding.

I decided we needed to give froggie some much deserved alone and safe time, so I got the dogs to follow me by sharing the treats in my pocket and we headed toward the house.

I shared my frog story with Mike later that night and the fact that I was worried about the little fella. But when the sun went down, I was happy to hear the bullfrog singing his song and knew he was safe from the killer bass ... and the silly little white dog.

Tattoo

It is no secret that I love my Sally. Some people have even said that I am a bit over-the-top with how I feel about this little white dog. What many people don't know is that Sally was my rescuer.

We got her to help my husband Mike with his grief after losing his nine-year old border terrier, Harry. They had been inseparable and when Harry died of cancer, Mike was inconsolable for months. When he started talking about getting a new dog, I was on board. He had always had a fondness for bull terriers. I thought they were ugly, but when he found Sally I did everything to facilitate getting her into Mike's arms. Including a flight from Kentucky.

I didn't think too much about this new little dog except the love and companionship she would provide for my husband. In my mind dogs were simply mess makers—droolers who ate disgusting things. My goal with Sally was to make Mike happier, and in doing so I was able to create a distraction from my own feelings of loss.

You see, a few months earlier my daughter Nicole had left home and moved away to college. It was a time of new beginnings for her and while my heart was breaking, my head was proud of her many achievements. My son Jacob was still in high school, but I knew the empty nest was looming. Loss would sneer at me when I passed Nicole's empty bedroom or set a place for her at the dinner table, but I tried my best to ignore these feelings.

Finally the day came when Sally would arrive at the airport in Grand Rapids. Mike was out of town, so I agreed to pick up the little dog. Peering into the carrier at the airport counter, those little black eyes staring back created a little flutter in my heart. And once I held her against me, I was head-over-heels-no-going-back in love.

Over the next few months of snuggling in bed, trips outside in the middle of the night for potty breaks, her sitting on my lap while I tried to work at my desk, along with disastrous experiences at puppy training class, Sally and I became insepa-rable. She brought joy into our lives, but none more than me.

Fast forward 10 years—Nicole has graduated from college and moved to New York with her boyfriend, while Jacob is moving to Los Angeles to pursue a career as a stand-up comedian. My empty nest echoes until my little whirling dervish runs into my room and slides across the floor, bumping into a wall. Her antics have filled my heart, three books and almost 90 articles in the *Cats and Dogs Magazine*. Jacob has even designed a Sally logo—which got me thinking, and one day I found myself walking into the Love Tattoo shop.

I am not a tattoo person, although I do find them an art form and am often intrigued by the tattoos people put on their bodies. I even some-times watch the tattoo shows on TV, but a tattoo on my body—never!

So as the tattoo artist, Preston, shows me the smaller version of the Sally logo and places it on the inside of my left ankle, my stomach is giddy. In fact, I'm trembling a little with excitement.

Preston tells me the cost and I reach for my wallet.

"Mom, I've got this," Jacob says. "I'm paying for your first tattoo."

I sit on the table while Preston gets everything ready and am surprised I am here. I had been thinking of doing this for months, but never thought I would do it.

"This is so emotional for me right now," I say, surprised at my unexpected tears. Jacob reaches over and touches my arm.

"Ready?" Preston asks. I nod and as the first drops of ink enter my skin I smile. It is a smile of happiness at sharing this new experience with Jacob, for Sally filling an empty spot in my life that I hadn't even acknowledged, and for all of the Sally experiences and people I have met over the past ten years.

When Preston finishes, I look at this little inked reflection and know that now I will always have my rescuer with me.

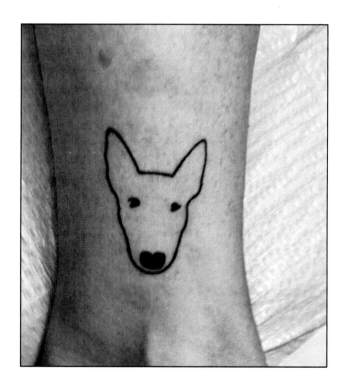

Naughty Sally

Sally naughty? No way! Maybe a little hard of hearing when she is being called but never naughty. That was my belief until an article titled The 10 Naughtiest Dog Breeds by Kelly Pulley caught my attention. Guess what breed was number two? The bull terrier. Say it isn't so!! But there it was in black and white—Bull Terrier. I felt a little better by the author's description of the breed as: "This energetic breed can have trouble with obsessive compulsive disorder, but its sense of humor is what one notices most."

Sally has a great sense of humor and at least once a day I am laughing at the little white dog. And yes, she does have some trouble with obsessive compulsive disorder on occasion, like when she is staring around the corner at the cat for hours, but naughty?

I continued reading and found the five characteristics of a naughty dog. Let's see if they fit Miss Sally.

1. Charisma. The author describes it as persuading everyone that you're doing what they want you to, even though you're not. Sally seems to spend a lot of time doing what she wants, and we just go along with it. Hmmm—I think that's a yes for Charisma.

2. Desire to Please. Here it states that naughty dogs want us to approve of their misbehaving. Since most of my articles about Sally revolve around some interesting (could it also be called naughty) Sally behaviors, I'm thinking this is also a check.

3. Willingness to Disobey. This is where the "I can't hear you calling my name over and over and over" comes into play. In fact, Sally will look right at me when I'm calling and then go back to whatever she is doing. Willingness to disobey—check!

4. Sense of (Canine) Humor. Sally wags her tail almost non-stop and when she isn't wagging it, she's chasing it. The author states that dogs laugh with their tails. I would say Sally is laughing her butt off.

5. A Sense of (Human) Humor. This is our perception of their behavior. Since I spend a lot of time laughing at Sally's antics, I would have to say this is another check. And this article is starting to make me think maybe it should be titled The 10 Naughtiest Dog Breed Owners.

At this point, the article moves on to Why Are Some Dogs Naughty? Should I continue reading? After all, we didn't do so well with the characteristics of a naughty dog.

1. To Get Attention. Really? Sally wants attention? This little dog has three books written about her for goodness sake. She gets more attention than the humans in the house. Wait, maybe that's the problem.

2. To Prove a Point. Okay, what point is Sally trying to make by licking every toad in the yard? Or stalking and (gulp) eating butterflies?

3. To Cheer You Up. The author states that not all dogs have this ability to empathize with humans, but many do. Sally definitely has this ability. If I'm sick, she's right there beside me, snuggling as close as possible. Of course now that I think about it, she's snuggling up with me even when I'm not sick. Perhaps she's just lazy? No way, she is just an expert when it comes to snuggling. I see that as intuitive. She knows what I need, when I need it. Apparently, I need lots of snuggling.

At last we get to The Difference Between "Naughty" and "In the Dog House." Uh oh!

1. Degree of Destruction. I don't see Sally as destructive, unless it is my yoga ball or a new toy and then it is destroyed within seconds. Of course maybe one of the toads soaked in Sally spit might see this differently.

2. Degree of Inconvenience. Sally can be annoying, not so much inconvenient. Although when she is ignoring me when I am telling her to stop eating something outside and then she comes into the house and pukes on the carpeting, that is bordering on inconvenient.

3. Degree of Danger. The only real danger is to butterflies and they seem to have learned not to land close to the little white dog's face, no matter how still she is standing.

So all in all, I would have to say that Sally is borderline naughty and most of that behavior happens in the summer months when we are outside. We get a reprieve in the winter due to her willingness to disobey when we want her to go outside in the snow. But who could blame her for that? Not me. And if I ever see an article titled The 10 Naughtiest Dog Breed Owners, I'm ignoring it. [Photo by Rachel Kay Photography]

Naughty Sally

Idiosyncrasy

Sally has some interesting idiosyncrasies—to say the least. She won't eat out of a bowl, and her food has to be poured out in a relatively straight line on a place mat. It is located in the laundry room/bathroom off the kitchen, and on some days it is necessary for someone (me) to be in the room with her while she eats. Otherwise she just follows me around the house and Eli takes this opportunity to run in and eat her food.

She also does not care for uncarpeted floors. This became evident when she was in her first puppy class. That floor was cement for obvious cleaning benefits, and Sally refused to get into the "down" position. It took the trainer and me a multitude of tries before we realized it was because she did not want her belly touching the cold floor. We put a rug in front of her and she did a perfect "down" for us. In our house, most of the floors are not carpeted so Sally runs from rug to rug—even if that means taking the extra long way around the room.

Knowing her penchant for peculiarity, I should be more cautious when I try something new with Sally, but sometimes I forget.

One evening I was in the bathroom getting ready for bed. I changed into my pajamas, washed my face, brushed my teeth and used a paper Dixie cup for a glass of water. That's when I noticed Sally standing on the bathroom rug and staring up at me. Normally she is only in the bathroom when I get out of the shower so she can lick my wet legs—another unconventional behavior. Therefore, I was curious as to what she wanted. She seemed to be staring at the cup in my hand so I filled it with water and held it down for her. She lapped at the water and just like that, a new Sally habit was born.

Every night after that was a similar routine— pajamas, wash face, brush teeth, and drink for Sally. She was a messy drinker so I always held the cup over the rug to keep the floor dry, and then stepped in that wet spot when I woke in the middle of the night for a trip to the toilet. Even so, it was a silly little thing that I didn't give much thought to until I noticed that every time I went into the bathroom, Sally followed me in and waited for a drink. She had replaced her water bowl with hand-delivered water. It was a new idiosyncrasy for the little white dog.

On one occasion, I was bent over giving Sally her nightly drink when Mike walked in. I quickly squashed the cup in my hand, spilling water on my feet, and walked nonchalantly to the waste basket.

"What were you just doing?" he asked, as he watched Sally licking my toes.

"Huh? Just getting ready for bed. Why?"

"Don't tell me you were giving Sally water out of a cup."

I fake laughed, but avoided answering him. He raised his eyebrow (I hate it when he does that), as I walked past and left the room.

After that I listened to see where he was in the house before I gave Sally her drink, but a couple days later, he busted me in the act again.

"Seriously?" He gave me a head tilt.

"What's the big deal?" I said. "It's just a cute little moment we share together."

"Mm hmm," he said, giving me a sympathetic look.

I made a face at him once he left the room.

After that I didn't even worry about him walking in and Sally's cup drinking continued. There were many occasions when I wondered why I had ever started this ridiculous routine, but for the most part it was just a new Sally quirk.

Then it happened. I walked into the bathroom and Mike was standing there with a Dixie cup in his hand and a guilty look on his face. In front of him on the rug were Sally ... and Eli.

"Eli, too?" I asked.

Mike nodded as he bent over and held the cup out for Eli, who lapped at it without spilling a drop.

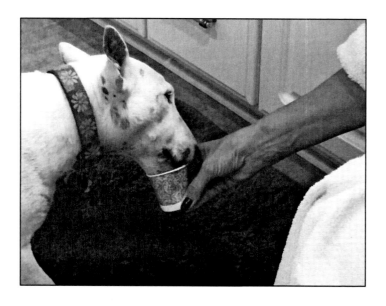

Sally's Boo Boo

It all started with a trouble-making bone.

Last weekend we visited friends who live about two hours south of our home. We took Eli and Sally with us, so I packed their overnight bag. Mike got the car ready by placing a blanket on the seat so their furry little behinds didn't slide around, even though they were seat-belted in. Being belted is something Sally still doesn't find amusing and she lets us know many times throughout the trip. I filled a couple of doggy chew toys with peanut butter and we were off.

I was looking forward to a quiet ride, but instead had to listen to the slurping noise of two doggy tongues licking peanut butter. Not a pleasant sound, but better than Sally's high-pitched car bark that comes out of nowhere and makes me jump. Eli managed to erase all remnants of peanut butter in a record-setting ten minutes. Then he started whining and whining and whining.

"What's the matter with him?" Mike asked.

"Do I look like the dog whisperer?" I asked. "I have no idea."

I reached backwards, almost dislocating my shoulder, and wiggled my fingers at Eli.

"It's okay, Buddy," I said. He whined while licking my fingers.

"Did you give him his composure meds?" Mike asked.

"I did, but I think another one won't hurt." I pulled out the bag from the doggy overnight bag. "Supports calm behavior and brain health," I read out loud. I held one out to Eli and he swallowed it. Sally lifted her face out of her chew toy and looked at us. Calm and Sally aren't often used in the same sentence, so I figured it would not hurt to "support calm behavior" in her, too. "Here you go, Sal."

The rest of the car ride was uneventful, except for a few Sally car barks after she finished her peanut butter. Eli was just chillin' and keeping an eye on Sally's chewy, just in case it rolled close enough for him to snatch it.

That evening, Sally played with Griffin, our friends' large German shepherd. At least Sally seemed to think it was playing. Griffin might have thought it was harassment. Sally would chase him around the table, and jump at his face.

Eli was not comfortable with the Griffin and Sally high-jinx. When Griffin started barking, which he did to get Sally to chase him, Eli would tremble. At one calm point, he ran over to Griffin's basket of toys (something we don't own because Sally destroys all toys within minutes), and grabbed a large raw-hide bone. It was pretty big, but he managed to climb onto the couch with it and start gnawing. The next morning when we got ready to leave, Griffin gave permission for Eli to take it home with him. Eli was happy, we were happy (quiet ride home), and Sally didn't care what was going on as long as she had her peanut butter.

Once we got home, we had to monitor the bone and make sure Sally didn't grab it away from Eli. She wasn't allowed to chew on hard things because of her teeth issues as she has already had several dental procedures, including a doggy root canal. It was better for Sally and our pocketbook if we made sure her mouth stayed away from hard things.

We were doing pretty well with bone control until Monday evening. Eli was chewing on the bone on his pillow in the living room and Sally and I were snuggling on the couch. When Mike came home, we went into the kitchen to welcome him. At least I thought all of us went in there.

Seconds later, I heard growling and snarling from the living room and found Eli and Sally in a nasty fight. The bone was lying on the pillow between them.

"Hey!" I yelled. They ignored me, so I took a step toward them and they separated. I grabbed the trouble-making bone and took it to the kitchen with Eli trotting along beside me, staring at it longingly. I put it in a cupboard out of sight. Looking around, I noticed Sally was not in the kitchen with us.

"Sally?" I walked back to the doggy pillow and there she sat with sad eyes and blood on her head. I picked her up, carried her to the bedroom and set her on the bed. The blood was coming from a couple bite marks on her ear.

"Poor Sally," Mike said, rubbing her back. With great Sally drama, she sighed and dropped onto her side.

We cleaned her ear and were relieved to see that she would not need stitches, so we gave her lots of kisses which she was happy to accept.

"Where's the little biter?" Mike asked as we looked around for Eli. "He probably feels bad."

"Yeah, right," I said, walking into the kitchen. There sat unrepentant Eli, staring at the cupboard with the bone.

Sally's Boo Boo

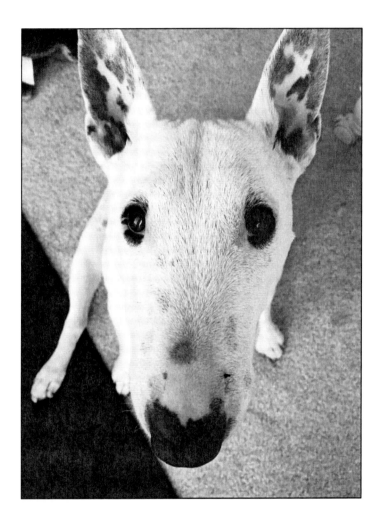

Pilates with Doggies

Sneaking down the stairs, I tip toe, stepping over the one stair that creaks, trying to make sure Eli and Sally don't hear where I am going. I stop at the bottom and listen, but don't hear any doggy scrabbling through the house. So far, so good.

I close the door with utmost care, making sure it doesn't slam shut.

In our exercise room, I sit on the bench and put my shoes on. I carried them with me to help reduce the sound of my footsteps so the dogs wouldn't be clued into where I was headed. Crossing the room, again on tip toe, I blow the dust off my exercise video and pop it into the DVD player. Looking at the three remotes, I pick what I think is the one for the DVD and hit On. The TV springs to life—blaring a commercial for a cleaning product. It is obvious the last time I was on the treadmill (a few months ago?) I didn't turn the volume down when I was done. I jab at buttons, trying to find mute and as soon as I find it, the door bangs open against the wall. They're here.

Eli dashes into the room first, with Sally hot on his heels. Even our 18-year-old-cat starts meowing at the top of his lungs, having felt the vibration of the door against the wall. Socks is pretty much deaf, but his vocals are louder now than they have ever been.

My shoulders slump as I look at the screen and see that my Pilates mat video has started, so I hit pause. It should say Pilates, plus two dogs and one cat.

I'm sure some would tell me to stop whining and take control of this situation. After all, I'm the human and they are mere pets. Control possibilities could be (1) Close and latch the door so they can't come in. The door has a glass panel and they sit on the other side and stare at me— sometimes even throwing in some whining; or, (2) Lock them in their kennels. Really? I feel bad enough when I have to put them in there when we're gone. Plus, they know I'm home and make sure I know they aren't happy.

My guess is that many of the people who would suggest some options are also individuals who do not have pets. If they did, they wouldn't even think such nonsense. They would understand the lack of control I possess when it comes to Sally.

Sighing, I roll my yoga mat onto the floor. Sally and Eli are now in a wrestling match and decide I have put this down for their benefit. Eli grabs Sally by the back of the leg and drags her over to the mat for a pin. Sally performs a body spin and knocks Eli over with a head butt. Socks sits on the bench licking his paw, watching the shenanigans.

I hit play, adjust the volume and drop to my mat, shooing the dogs away. I roll down onto my back and start with The Hundred. I get to about 13 when I receive the first doggy lick attack—one on each side of my face. My hands are working at my sides, so I shoo the lickers away with a violent head movement. I focus on the exercise and ignore them, but Eli is not dissuaded, as is evidenced by the paw in my face move. He is lying beside my head, so I try to shove him away but now he is pulling the dead weight routine. By the time he is gone, the video has moved to Single Leg Stretch.

I roll my head and shoulders up off the mat and stretch my legs in and out, counting each movement. At the end, I am happy I was able to get through the whole exercise without any animal distraction. Unrolling onto the mat, the back of my head lands on a fur pillow, thanks to Socks.

"Come on, you guys," I say, a whine in my voice that disgusts even me. Sally thinks this is a call to action, so she runs over to Socks and starts annoying him. He runs away and it appears across my body is the easiest route, with Sally close on his heels. I clutch at my stomach, and then turn my head toward the sound of running water. "Eli!" He stops mid-pee and gives me the Who, me? look.

I pause the video, shoo the dogs outside in the snow, grab paper towels and clean up the warm pee (ugh) before anyone has a chance to track it through the house. I let the maniacs back in, wash my hands and lay back down on my mat—which I find is now covered in melting snow. "Really? All I want to do is exercise," I say. My whining meter is rising.

I push through Double Leg Stretch and even The Roll Up, dodging doggy tongues and Socks' tail flicking across my face. But when Sally walks over and stands on my chest, I decide enough is enough. After all, ten minutes of actual exercise is better than nothing, right?

I roll onto my side and Sally curls into me. Eli stretches out along my legs and Socks wanders off toward his bowl. I manage a few Side Leg Stretches before I change the channel and we finish my work-out routine watching the morning news—on the floor together.

The Shortest Route
is Not Always
the Easiest

"What is she doing?" my friend Gloria asks as Sally runs past the kitchen where Gloria is standing.

"She is actually coming over to say hi," I say, "but she has her own route."

It should come as no shock to anyone who knows Sally, that she has some interesting idiosyncrasies. I am thankful for each and every one of those unconventional behaviors because without them, writing about her would have become boring long ago. The fact that I still have new things to write after over 100 articles is pretty amazing.

Believe it or not, I have had people tell me she is downright crazy, to which I reply, "She's not crazy, she's quirky." I think my husband is one of those people who say she is crazy—but it is never said around her.

One of her peculiarities is that she does not like walking on hardwood floors. Sally has thick nails so she tends to slip on wood floors. This may be common for many dogs, although I have only seen it in action with Sally.

So what do you do when you don't like walking on wood floors? You find a way of NOT walking on them. For Sally it means we have a lot of rugs in the house and she makes her own paths.

Our bedroom is carpeted, but the kitchen is not. Therefore, when she leaves the bedroom she runs straight across the room to the back door, where there is a rug. Depending on her ultimate destination, she may just go outside from this point. Getting her to this spot is often a challenge since she has to give a lot of thought, along with many starts and stops, before she will leave the safety of the bedroom carpet and venture onto the wood floor.

If she does not want to go outside, she takes a right hand turn and runs down the hallway (wooden floor) to the front door and another rug. This is an area rug which is quite large so she is happy when she gets there. She expresses this with a couple of happy spins.

If she is headed outside but didn't want to go out the back door (for whatever Sally reason is percolating in that little head of hers), she now goes out the front door. Coming in this door is challenging since she hesitates if the rug is not right up to the edge of the doorway. After all, she might slip on that three inch spot of wood.

If her goal was not to go outside, she turns right again and runs to the living room where the floor is an uneven slate and there is no slipping or sliding. This room used to be carpeted, but Eli seemed to think that living room also meant bathroom, so we had to tear it all out. We spent a great deal of time and consideration into what we would replace it with, and much of that thought included what Eli would not destroy and what Sally would walk on.

If you are now thinking that having dogs is a lot like having toddlers that never grow up, you are the owner of a dog or dogs.

Sally has now made it to the slate floor and if this was her destination, she stretches out on the pillow in front of the fireplace or settles onto the couch. Her favorite place is the overstuffed chair in the corner surrounded by windows, but only if there is a lap for her to cuddle into.

On this particular evening, this was not Sally's final endpoint. Her mission was to get to

Gloria to give and get some love. That meant going through the dining room and more of that dreaded hardwood floor.

Standing at the edge of where the slate met the wood, she gathered her resolve by backing up and stepping forward several times. She even threw in a couple little whines before she overcame her hesitation and burst across the dining room floor, into the kitchen and onto the rug in front of the sink. Eureka—she made it to Gloria!

She travelled approximately 65 feet to get to what would have been less than 10 feet, just so she could move from rug to rug and avoid the dreaded hardwood floor.

At that point, Mike walked in the back door and Sally turned and ran back through the dining room, over the slate floor to the area rug, down the hallway and into the arms of her dad. Whew! With all that running, it is no wonder this little white dog is in such good shape!

Ugh!

Warning: This story may not be suitable for all readers (especially those with weak stomachs).

I received the news via an email from Ingrid, our groomer. She had been at our house earlier that day, while I was out, and had given Eli and Sally their baths and clipped their nails. She had sent the email while she was with them, but I was just now reading it –

Not 100% sure as I had already started wetting her down, but I think I just pulled a tapeworm off Sally's butt.

I gagged on my soup, put my spoon down and read it again. Ugh! I sent an email back -

Gross!! What does that mean? Could she have more? Should we take her to the vet? I've never dealt with tapeworms before.

As I waited for her reply, I dumped the rest of my soup in the garbage. I had lost my appetite. I heard the familiar ding, signifying a new email -

Yep, a fecal to the vet. They get them if they ingest a flea or dead animal. Wasn't totally sure though since I was rinsing her.

I wrote back - *We have a vet appointment for the dogs tomorrow, so I'll make sure we take a fecal with us. Thank you for letting me know.*

My stomach did a couple more flips. I was going to give Mike the job of retrieving that fecal sample. Ding –

For sure. They need to be super fresh and even then those things don't always show up. I wish I could be more sure. I didn't see any on Eli. They're easier to find on dogs with bushy rears like Eli.

Super fresh fecals? Bushy rears? This was more information than I needed and when Sally came up to me for touches, I made sure I kept my hand away from her rear. Bushy or not—I was not going anywhere near it.

Before we left for the vet appointment the next morning, I told Sally to "take care of business" and off she went. Normally she would go into the outside kennel area, but not today. Instead she walked through the brush and dead branches, deep into the woods. I grabbed the plastic bag from Mike's hand as I headed in after her.

"I already turned it inside out," he said.

"Gee, thanks," I said under my breath.

I stopped where Sally had been squatting and picked up the feces (with the gloved hand), turned the bag right side out and sealed it.

"There's a white worm on her poop!" I said, holding the bag at arm's length. I would have said more, but I was gagging again. Mind you, I'm the mother of two grown children so I have had my share of dealing with unpleasant body excrements, but poop has always had a way of making me retch. And this was no exception.

Handing the bag to Mike, we looked at it through the safety of the sealed plastic.

"It definitely looks like a tapeworm," he said. "See how it flattens out."

I left him peering at the bag, went inside and washed my hands over and over. At the car, I buckled the dogs into the back seat and off we went to the vet's office. After running a test, Dr. Heidi informed us that, "Yes, Sally has a tape-worm."

We asked her a lot of questions about how Sally might have gotten it—from eating some-thing dead out in the woods, no doubt—and how she would get rid of them. Dr. Heidi told us that once the worms leave the body, they die right away and they often looked like dried up pieces of rice.

My stomach lurched as I remembered cleaning little pieces of rice off the downstairs couch where Sally and I always sat together. *Who was eating Chinese food in here?* I had thought. That meant those little worms were crawling out of her…I didn't like where my thoughts were heading so I stopped thinking. We drove home with medication and a warning that Sally might throw up the worms because she had so many. Ugh!

The rest of the day passed without any puking incidents (mine or Sally's) and I managed to put the tapeworm thoughts out of my head until I was getting ready for bed. Sally always slept under the covers and that meant…I pulled the blankets back and there they were…hundreds, if not thousands (slight exaggeration for impact), of tiny little dried up pieces of rice-looking dead tapeworms.

I dropped the blankets, backed into the bathroom and stood over the toilet trying to breathe normally.

I heard Mike walk into the bedroom and I returned, lifted the blankets, and said, "Look." He started brushing the tiny carcasses onto the floor.

"Just think," he said. "While you were sleeping, these little worms were probably crawling all over you."

"Stop," I said.

"There are so many," he laughed. "I'm surprised you never felt any of them creeping and crawling on your legs."

"Mike, I'm serious. Quit."

I pulled the sheets off the bed, stuffed them into the washing machine and that night, I slept wearing socks, a long sleeved shirt and sweatpants.

Eli's Turkey

"Sally! Come on booda," I called as I stumbled through the woods. Sally had been missing for almost 30 minutes and my sister Joyce and I were searching the wooded area around our house. "Sally, treats!" I stopped and listened, longing for the tinkling sound of the dog license hanging from her collar. I was on the verge of panic, still telling myself she was just being a brat and not listening to me.

As I started walking again, my foot caught on a thorny vine. "Ouch," I said, as it scratched at my bare toe. Sandals were not the smart foot-wear accessory for the woods, but I hadn't anticipated spending my afternoon scrambling through brush and dead trees. I licked my finger and wiped at the blood seeping from the scratch. As I did so, I thought I heard movement straight ahead. "Sally!" I could see some white in the distance, but it wasn't moving. My heart started racing as I wondered if that was Sally, why she wasn't moving. *Is she hurt?* I crashed through the brush faster, calling her name and saw the white blob move to the right a little. That was her alright and the little brat was just ignoring me.

When I reached her she looked up at me, a black feather hanging out of her mouth. I looked around and saw she had found the turkey—the dead turkey. To understand this story better, I need to give you some background information.

The morning before, as Sally and I were still snuggled under the covers, Mike rushed into the bedroom.

"Eli's missing," he said.

"What?" I said, throwing the covers off. Sally blinked at me with annoyance.

"He's been gone for about 30 minutes." Mike grabbed his shoes out of the closet as he headed back out the door.

I grabbed my mangy, but oh-so-comfy robe from the hook in the bathroom and put it on as I followed Mike. He jumped in the car and raced down the driveway as I walked around the yard. "Eli! Come on, Eli. Suppies!" The suppies word usually always works, so when it didn't work after several attempts, I started to worry. I heard dogs barking in the distance and listened to see if it was Eli's bark. It wasn't, but I wondered if maybe they were barking at Eli.

I saw Mike driving up and down our two-track road until he drove back up to the house and parked in the garage.

"The last time I saw him he was just up there," Mike said pointing, "where he always goes to take care of his business."

"Eli!"

We walked away from the house and down the driveway, calling and calling. During a break in our voices, I thought I heard the sound of his collar and turned toward the house. Eli was standing near the garage.

"Mike, there he is," I said. "And he has something in his mouth."

"What is it?"

"I'm not sure, but it looks dead."

Mike and I walked toward the killer, aka Eli.

"Eli, drop it," Mike said. Eli dropped the dead thing on the pavement and we both bent over to get a good look.

"Gross! It's a turkey head and neck," I said. "He chased down and killed a turkey."

"No."

I checked Eli over and he didn't have any scrapes, scratches or blood on him so we guessed he hadn't been the killer in this case.

"What do we do with it?" Mike asked.

"Put it in a Ziplock® and throw it in the garbage." I went in the house to grab a plastic bag, and then handed it to Mike.

"You do it," he said.

"Ugh, no."

"Why do I have to do it?"

"Because." I really couldn't come up with a better answer, so Mike grabbed the bag and walked toward the head carcass.

When we were all back in the house we checked Eli over again and the only thing we found on him was a very full belly.

"Guess he doesn't need breakfast today," I said.

That brings me to the point in my story where I am looking at Sally standing in the middle of a pile of turkey feathers. "No," I yelled as she bent toward a scrawny, kind-of-creepy looking turkey leg. Looking around I realized there wasn't much left of the turkey, so it must have been feasted on by a myriad of creatures over the past day and night.

"Joyce, I found her," I called as I shooed Sally toward the house and we stumbled back through the tree debris. "Oh, and I found Eli's turkey, too."

Eli's Turkey

The Cone of Shame

"There is no way Sally is going to wear a cone," Mike says after I tell him about our visit to the vet.

"That's what I told them," I say. "But they said that I would be surprised how fast dogs adjust to them."

"Did you tell them that Sally isn't a normal dog? She won't even eat out of a bowl? We have to pour her food in a straight line on a mat shaped like a bone on the floor, remember?"

A few days earlier our daughter Nicole had been feeding the dogs and she poured Sally's food in the empty water dish in the bathroom. "That's not where Sally's food goes," I said.

"Well, what bowl does it go in then?" she asked, looking around the room.

"It doesn't go in a bowl; you just spread it out on that mat."

Nicole raised her eyebrows in that 'you know you're crazy, right?' look, so I left the room.

The day after our cone conversation, Mike and I drive to the vet's office to pick Sally up from her surgery. She had a growth on the back of her leg that was removed and the biopsy will be sent in for testing to see if it is cancerous. Mike drives so I can hold Sally on my lap on the drive home. He knows the rest of the evening will be spent with me snuggling Sally as much as possible.

After talking with Dr. Moore, we go in the back to get Sally. She is pretty woozy still and "eeek" she is wearing the cone of shame. I am embarrassed for her. We take it off for the ride home and since I don't let Sally out of my sight, it stays off until the following day—Saturday.

About mid-day I decide that I really need to get outside and take care of a few chores, but I don't want Sally hobbling behind me. That means I have to put the cone of shame on her.

"It's only for a little while," I say as I slip it over her head. I pull her ears forward and loosely tie the cone around her neck. I set her on her pillow and stifle a laugh as I turn and walk away. I sneak a look over my shoulder as she stumbles toward me, the bottom of the cone banging on the carpet. Each time it hits the floor, she comes to an abrupt halt.

"Just stay on your pillow," I say to her, but she continues to bump her way toward me. I slip out the door and then peek in through the window. She is standing just inside the bedroom staring at the door I just walked out of.

I rush through my chores and 45 minutes later, I hurry into the house to see how the patient has done. She is standing in the exact same spot inside the bedroom, still staring at the door. It doesn't look like she has moved at all. Adjusting to the cone is not going well.

Two days later I have to leave the house for some appointments, so I slide the cone back over Sally's head and unfold her ears again. I offer her a treat and she turns her coned head to the side, bumping it against my leg.

"Oh Sally, it is okay," I say. She continues to refuse my attempt at bribery. Several hours later I pull into the driveway and look at the front door. Sally is looking out the window, cone in place, and I burst out laughing. I feel guilty at my outburst but really, she looks ridiculous.

Over the days following her surgery, Sally wears her cone of shame whenever I am gone, although I admit I rearrange my schedule on a few days so I don't have to leave her. She always comes to me when I call her, even though I have the cone in my hand, and she even starts to take the bribery treat I offer. I consider this a cone victory.

While on my way home on the fifth day, I listen to a voicemail from Dr. Moore. They received the biopsy report and it is clean!! I hurry into the house and Sally runs toward me. I pick her up and the cone bangs into my cheek and then my forehead, but I don't mind. I am so happy I would even wear the cone for Sally. Not really—at least not in public.

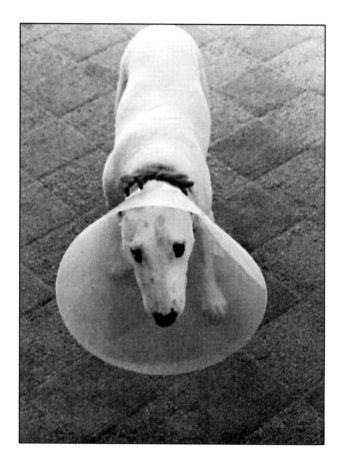

Eli & Sally Differences

I was talking with a friend the other day about the difference, if any, between rescued and non-rescued dogs. We came to the conclusion that rescues seem more grateful for everything. Since we have one of each—our non-rescue Sally, a mini bull terrier, and our rescue Eli, a Jack Russell/Australian cattle dog—I decided to see if that was true in our circumstance.

Feeding –

As we pour food into Eli's bowl, he stands to the side and wiggles with excitement. He then looks up at us with a thank you before he digs in.

Sally refuses to eat out of a bowl, and scrutinizes us as pour her food in a straight line on her food mat. She then dismisses us as she starts to eat. After all, it is her food and she is allowing us to serve her.

Bedtime –

Eli waits in his kennel until both Mike and I are in bed and call him. He then jumps onto the bed, walks to the middle of the pillows; gives Mike a few thank you licks and curls into a ball.

Sally gives me the evil eye until I pick her up and place her on the bed. Once I get in, she dives under the blankets and slams her body against mine until I move over. After all, it is her bed and she is allowing us to sleep with her.

Sitting on the couch –

Eli curls into one end of the couch, careful not to disturb where we are sitting. If we invite him to sit close to us, he slides in gently.

If we are sitting too close to Sally's end of the couch, she gives us her evil eye until we move over and beg her to sit with us. If the eye action doesn't work, she'll provide a couple of sharp little yaps to get our attention. After all, it is her couch and she is allowing us to sit with her.

Riding in the car –

We put Eli in his harness; he jumps into the backseat and waits for us to buckle him into the seatbelt.

As we put Sally's harness on her, she wiggles in an attempt to thwart our actions. When we get her into the car, she runs to the opposite side of the seat to avoid the seatbelt. Once we strap her in, she stares at the front seat, barking to express her disgust at having to be confined to the back. After all, it is her car and she is allowing us to drive her around.

Obedience –

When we call Eli, he stops and turns to look at us. We call him again and he comes running. He sometimes gets distracted on the way, but his intention is to come when called.

If Sally is walking away from us and we call her, she continues on her way. If we call her name a second time, she will pause and turn with an annoyed look. She then keeps going in the opposite direction. After all, it is her world and we are lucky she allows us to live in it with her.

Is Sally Just a Furry Toddler?

Toddlers are often defined as "completely unpredictable" and "prone to selective hearing." Having survived the toddler years with my two now-grown children, I realize that owning a dog is like having a toddler that never grows up.

A ringing telephone to a toddler means that mom's attention is not going to be on them—time to change that. Sally can be sleeping in another room and as soon as she hears me on the phone she searches me out. If I'm sitting in a chair, she has to get up on my lap. If she can't get onto my lap by herself, she will bump my arm continuously with that crazy nose of hers until I put the phone down and pull her onto said lap. If I'm walking around, she has to follow close enough to trip me, or run into my legs when I stop.

Company to a toddler means it is time to be entertaining so, once again, all the attention is on them. When I have a client at my office/home, Sally will stand beside the table and bark. She will also sneak under the table and lick the leg/ankle of said client. She will tap dance on the hardwood floor to create a noise distraction. If that doesn't work, she will spin—stop—then spin again until we quit what we are doing and comment on her.

I had to resort to putting her in another room and shutting the door because she was such a pest. That resulted in the most pitiable alien-like noises EVER coming from that crack underneath the door.

Toddlers expect that you will know what they want, when they want it, and provide whatever it is to them. Sally will sit by the front door and stare at it. We may not even know she is there, but she will continue to sit. If no one opens the door in what she considers a timely manner, she will move to a standing position and continue to stare. Should we still not read her mind, she will emit one bark. Not a series of barks, as those are saved for the UPS man.

Once we hear that one bark, we are expected to stop whatever we are doing and open the door so she can go out—maybe. Sometimes she just looks out the open door, and then decides she doesn't really want to go out—yet. She is guaranteed to change her mind once I get back to whatever I was doing in the first place.

Toddlers are notoriously picky eaters. I don't have to go into too much detail about Sally here. Just know that she won't eat her food out of a bowl. It has to be poured—in a straight line, not dumped into a pile—on a bone-shaped red/white mat. She would also prefer to drink water from a small cup held by a human, rather than a bowl on the floor. Enough said.

A toddler can hear the sound of a phone ringing in a different level of a house, but not your voice beside them. When Sally is outside and out of my sight, I just yell "Sally, no" over and over until she reappears. I don't even need to see what she is doing to know she shouldn't be doing it.

If Sally is playing out in the yard and starts wandering away from me, I'll call her name and she will pause, and then continue on her way. She won't even look back at me. However, if I quietly open a food package across the yard, in a wind storm, she will hear it and make a mad dash toward me. They call it selective hearing.

And lastly, when a toddler falls asleep, they often look angelic and there is peace and tranquility in the room. When I look at Sally curled into my lap, or snuggling beside me on the couch, I find myself emitting a big happy sigh that carries me through to the next time she trots away from me using her selective hearing.

Sleeping with Dogs

I knew we were in trouble as soon as I saw the size of the bed in the cottage. It wasn't a king like the one we shared at home. It wasn't even a queen like the one in the guest room where Sally and I would slip off to when my night sweats kept me awake. No, it was a full—the size between a twin and a queen. In other words, it was not big enough for me, my husband, Sally and Eli. It meant someone was not going to get any sleep, and I knew that someone was going to be me.

Mike went to bed first because he didn't want to suffer through watching The Voice with me. He was switching back and forth between that and the Monday Night Football game, but after he missed a great play by his favorite player on his favorite team, he sulked off to bed. The dogs stayed with me on the couch and about 90 minutes later, we followed.

First though, was a "take care of business" trip outside for the dogs. They both scrambled down the stairs of the porch and Eli got right to it, and then bounded back into the house. Sally had to wander around first, looking for the perfect spot to squat.

"Come on, Sally," I said. She ran back to the porch and lifted one paw. "Sally, let's go." Since the wind was blowing and there was a light rain, I stood just inside the door. She stepped back off the step. I walked out onto the wet porch in my socks.

"Sally, I mean it, get in here," I said, using my stern voice. She walked back and forth, then put a paw on the step again and paused. She was having one of her nervous moments and for some reason, known only to her, she was nervous about the steps she had just bounded down.

I walked farther out onto the landing, feeling the rain soak into my pajamas. "Damn it, Sally. I don't have time for your craziness tonight."

After a few more minutes of back and forth, she scampered up the steps, into the house and made a beeline for the bedroom. By now, Eli was already laying between Mike and one side of the bed. Sally stood silent, waiting for me to lift her onto the bed. Which, of course I did. I then climbed in, or at least I tried to climb in. Mike had moved his legs to my side of the bed to give Eli more room, which meant that my tiny third of the bed was now more like a fourth of the bed. I wiggled under the covers and Sally forced herself between Mike and me. She kept trying to circle and find a good spot, but there wasn't enough room so she kept stepping on me. I rolled onto my side and scootched over. Now I was hanging off the bed but at least Sally was able to get comfortable.

I layed like this for about 30 minutes, trying to sleep without falling off the bed. I even managed to roll onto my back, although I still couldn't stretch my legs out because of Mike's legs. The moment came when I was just drifting off into dreamland and Mike's elbow rammed into my neck. Really? He had rolled onto his back and put his hands under his head. I shoved his arm out of the way.

"Mike," I whispered. No response. "Mike!" I repeated a bit louder. "Sally and I are going to sleep on the couch," I said. "And we're taking the comforter with us."

"Okay," he said. I don't think he realized what was going on until I started tugging on the blanket. Eli tumbled toward the edge of the bed and I tried to catch him, but he was playing possum and fell on the pile of bedding on the floor. Back onto the bed, he scampered to my empty pillow.

I grabbed Sally, along with a pillow, and left the bedroom, trailing the comforter behind us. I made the couch into a makeshift bed by removing some of the cushions and I snuggled in. Sally paced on the couch bed until I realized she was afraid of the wind whistling through the sliding glass door.

Out of bed, I tried shutting the door tighter. Didn't work. I opened and closed it three times. Still whistling. I grabbed a chair and pushed it against the frame. This worked, but the sound of the chair moving scared Sally and she was now hiding in the kitchen.

It took some coaxing, but at last we were back in our little makeshift bed, snuggled under the blankets, and Sally was curled into my side, already snoring. I was ready for some well-deserved sleep when the whistling started again.

No Rest for Sally (or me)

Tina, my sister's dog, never walks—she bounces in a happy-go-lucky way that makes you smile.

"Tina's here!" I say as I open the front door and the cute little dog turns into a yappy creature. She runs to Sally and jumps on her face. Sally ducks and weaves her way around the little six-pound mass of white fur, but Tina sticks to her like a piece of lint.

My sister, Tina's mom, is going to Florida for a week and we have invited Beenie (Tina's alias) to stay with us. I haven't told the dogs (or Socks) the news for fear they would hide in the basement. Let's just say Beenie has a lot of energy that tires us out in a short period of time.

For our first overnight, Mike is out of town (convenient for him) and I put Sally onto the bed as per our routine. Then I pick up Tina and put her on the bed—not part of our routine, as Sally reminds me with the look of scorn on her face. I climb in and lift the sheets so Sally can slip underneath. Tina watches with curiosity and then walks on top of the Sally lump. Once there, she starts her yapping—oops, sorry, barking—which is an ear-splitting sharp yip that makes you want to jab something into your ear. That might be a slight exaggeration—but not much.

"Tina, please," I say and she quiets.

I shut off the bedside lamp and feel the mattress give way as Eli jumps onto it with a soft thud. Tina greets him with a new round of yapping.

Eli settles into the pillow and Sally burrows beside me. I pat the bed and call Tina to my side where she lays on top of the blankets. All is calm as I close my eyes and it is pretty restful. I face the remaining five nights with hope. My bad!

The second night we discover that two humans and three dogs in the same bed creates chaos, so Sally, Beenie and I head to the guest room. We follow the same routine, minus Eli's presence, and I am looking forward to a good night's sleep. Beenie has other ideas. Once the light goes off, she turns into night security. Every time Sally or I turn over or move, Beenie growls.

This goes on all night and repeats itself for the next two nights.

On the fourth night, Mike offers to keep Tina overnight and I agree with great enthusiasm. Perhaps too much enthusiasm as he tries to back out of the offer throughout the day. Sally and I share a secret smile all day thinking about the sleep we will get that night. We even go to bed early in anticipation, yet throughout the night I have nightmares of Tina scratching at the bedroom door and making odd alien noises from the next room. There is no restful sleep and when I emerge from the bedroom the next morning I find a bedraggled Mike and Eli sitting on the couch.

"How did it go last night?" I ask.

"Well, let me fill you in," he says with a sigh. "I put her on the bed, but she kept jumping off. Then she ran out of the room so I followed her and found her scratching on your door. I tried to grab her, but she darted into the other bedroom and ran under the bed." He took a breath. "I got down on my hands and knees, which wasn't a pretty sight, but I couldn't reach her."

Mike, myself, Sally and Eli are all crowded together on the couch staring at Tina, who is wagging her tail with great enthusiasm.

At some point during the next night's fiasco, Sally lies beside me with her head on the pillow.

Tina is sniffing at Sally's face. Sally looks at me with eyes that seem to say, "Really?"

"I know, I'm sorry, Sally," I say. "Only one more night."

At last it is Tina's final night with us. I have kept her busy all day, hoping she will fall into an exhausted sleep. I even stay up late—trying anything that might give us a night of much needed rest. After the obligatory growling and barking (by Tina, not me), my plan seems to be working as she settles down. Two hours later I wake to her little nose sniffing at my face. I push her away and she returns. We repeat this dance for several minutes, until I get up and take her outside. It is now 2:30am and the fresh air seems to have revitalized the little dog. The rest of the night is a fitful attempt at sleep—mostly unattainable. I stumble into the kitchen at 7:00am and find that Mike has already left for work. He calls moments later.

"Congratulations," he says.

"Why?"

"You made it through your last night with Beenie. How was it?"

"Horrible," I say. Tina bounces around my feet waiting for breakfast and her cute little face makes me smile—until Sally walks by and Tina starts yapping—again.

No Rest for Sally (or me)

Sally the Nursemaid

Tis' the season for lots of illnesses floating around, just waiting to invade someone and make them miserable for a few days or more. That happened to me recently and I found that Sally was a pretty good nurse—for a while.

Started with a scratchy throat that was intermittent over two days and nights. I figured it was allergies because it would come and go, never camping out. The day the cough and fever moved in, I knew I needed to sit back (or lay down) and just take it easy. Sally loved that idea.

Grabbing my favorite blanket (mine and Sally's), I moved to the family room. After arranging a glass of water, my iPad, and a few Sally treats onto the end table, I settled into the recliner end of the couch. It took Sally about 2.5 seconds to join me. She positioned herself between me and the arm of the couch, and I covered us with the blanket. Life was good—except for the aggressive coughing, but Sally didn't seem to notice.

I watched TV, checked Facebook and my emails, sent some texts and even napped a little. Later in the afternoon, Mike brought me a bowl of homemade chicken noodle soup. Turned out my appetite wasn't affected by my sickness, and before the end of the day I ate two more bowls. I even let Sally drink some of the broth when I was finished. She deserved a reward for being such a great companion. She spent the entire day snuggled in with me, except for a couple of potty breaks (for her and me).

That night, we slept in the guest room so we wouldn't keep the boys (Mike and Eli) awake with my coughing. Sally happily followed me into the room and jumped onto the bed. As usual, she wiggled under the blankets and we fell asleep—woke with coughing—fell back to asleep—awake with Sally rearranging—coughing again—more sleep—potty break for Sally—back to bed—more coughing. Needless to say, it was fitful night.

The next day, I dragged myself to the couch again. Mike went to work and I stayed on the recliner, Sally by my side. We were both so exhausted; we spent most of the morning napping. Socks even managed to sneak onto my lap while I was sleeping. When I woke, Sally was snoring, Socks was purring on my lap, and Eli was talking in his sleep beside me. No wonder I was awake.

My coughing continued and now Sally was noticing. Every time I coughed, she turned her head and looked at me. It was not a look of love.

The following night and day were more of the same sleeping pattern and schedule. However, on the third night in the guest room, Sally decided she had had enough and let me know. My coughing was starting to let up a little, so I was getting more sleep, which I desperately needed. Sally woke at 4:00 am and started fussing. First I thought something was wrong because Sally loves to snuggle and sleep. Now she was out of the covers, under, then back and forth under the blankets, back out to sit on the pillow beside my head. She tried rearranging the pillows, with my head still on it, which resulted in her standing on my face. This was not going well.

I let her outside, thinking she might have to take a pee break. While outside in the 35 degree wind, she decided it would be a good time to wander and ignore my voice. I had to walk out in my bare feet and get right beside her before she even looked up at me. I was not happy.

Back in the house, she headed for the master bedroom. "No Sally," I whispered. "This way." She went to her water bowl and started drinking (I use the word loosely) a ridiculous amount of water—I think some of it even got into her mouth. I had to drag her away from the bowl, which meant I also stepped in a big puddle of water.

At last I coaxed her to the guest room and back in bed, where she positioned herself next to my legs and I started to doze off. Not so for the little white dog. She bolted out of the covers and hung off the end of bed, staring at the door. Since I didn't get up and attend to the princess, she jumped off the bed and laid on a pillow on the floor. That is where she stayed until morning, when I finally dragged myself out of bed.

The next day Sally let me know that she was done with my being sick and I needed to buck up and get back to normal life. No more snuggling for inordinate amounts of time on the couch, and no more sleeping in the guest room. That night we were back in bed with Mike and Eli, where Sally stretched out under the covers in the middle—right where the princess belonged.

I hope I don't get sick again or I'll be very lonely.

Sally the Nursemaid

Rescued

Recently, my company, Splattered Ink Press, partnered with Cats and Dogs Magazine and published <u>Celebrating Animal Rescue</u>. It is a collection of short stories by writers across the United States about the experience of animal rescue.

As I worked on this book, I started thinking about my own experience with animal rescue. Growing up, our pets were disposable. I never had a senior animal, as they were always "disposed" of before they reached an older age. If a dog didn't behave, we turned them in and got a new one. I don't think my parents were even cognizant of the impression they were making on me as they also grew up with disposable pets. My mother told me a story of how, growing up on a farm, they had two pigs she named Spic and Span. She thought of them as her pets until she came home from school one day to find them skinned and hanging in the barn. Just the story was traumatizing to me and I can't imagine the emotional devastation she must have felt.

I continued the revolving door of pet ownership into my adult life until I met my husband, Mike and his bull mastiff, Jesse. I know it sounds ridiculous, but through their relationship I realized that pets were living, breathing beings—not things you tossed out when you tired of them. Even as I type this I am amazed at my lack of awareness at that time.

Since my awakening, as I call it, I have walked several pets through the normal life and death cycle. Their journeys have been exhilarating and unbelievably painful, but I feel honored to have shared our lives with them. Most of these pets were rescues, but a few were not, and one of those is Sally.

Sally is not a rescue. In fact, we did everything wrong when we purchased her. We found her online, we didn't check her parentage, we didn't go see her (she was in Kentucky), and we bought her through a second-party individual. Everything worked out okay and other than her many idiosyncrasies, we have a healthy dog, but it could have been a disaster.

Although Sally is not a rescue, I believe she rescued me. My life was changing when Sally came into our lives. My oldest child was living away at college and I knew my youngest would be doing the same in a short period of time. I was also in the middle of changing my career and felt uneasy and terrified that I would fail. My husband was dealing (or not) with depression over losing his dog, Harry, and my world was off-kilter. Everything around me was changing and not in a good way (that's how it felt at the time).

Then I pulled a little white dog, soaking wet from pee, out of her kennel at the airport and was swept off my feet. I truly believe she and I started bonding at that moment. I talked about her so much that Janet (editor of Cats and Dogs Magazine) asked me to write a monthly column about Sally for the magazine. From those stories, I self-published *Life With Sally Little White Dog Tails* and my son designed the cover. From there we formed Splattered Ink Press and started helping other writers publish their books. I also started coaching individuals who wanted to write, taught writing classes, gave presentations to adults and children in various settings, started two senior citizen writing classes, and created four writing conferences. This is only the tip of the iceberg as it doesn't even include all the amazing people I have met through this journey that continues day-to-day.

Who knew I would be rescued by a little white dog with a big personality.

A Little
White Dog Scare

It began with getting her teeth cleaned. This was done every 6-12 months as Sally has terrible teeth—maybe related to the fact that everything goes into her mouth. Not unlike a teething child. We are used to the call from Dr. Moore stating that she needed extra dental work, so when he called and said everything looked good, we were ecstatic.

I showed up at 5:00 pm to get her and, albeit a little dopey from the anesthesia, she was happy and ready to go home. In the parking lot I picked her up and put her in the car. By the time I got around to the other side, she had passed out. Running back in with her, Dr. Moore and his tech started checking her vitals. I leaned against the table while hyperventilating and feeling a bit woozy. Perhaps they should have checked my vitals, too.

Everything seemed okay, but they suggested I leave her there for a couple of hours so they could keep an eye on her. That made perfect sense, so I returned at 7:00 pm and there was Sally, wagging her tail and happy to see me. Dani (a vet tech) picked her up and I was giving Sally kisses when she passed out again. Was it me? Were my kisses too much?

The next hour or so was spent checking and re-checking her vitals, taking chest x-rays, and wondering what was going on. It was agreed that she seemed okay again, but we should consider taking her to the ER in Grand Rapids if she had any additional episodes that night. We headed home. I was hyper-vigilant watching every move she made in the car and once we got to the house. She went potty outside and followed me in the kitchen where I saw her wobble.

"Mike, she's going down again," I said, in a not-calm voice.

I grabbed her, ran into the bedroom and laid her on the bed. Mike talked to her in a soothing voice, stroking her head and after about a minute, she started to come to again. We took her to the ER vet in Grand Rapids; however they couldn't find anything and suggested we take her to MSU the next day. Knowing she was not in danger of dying as she never stopped breathing during these events, we took her home where she passed out yet again. This time Mike held her in the rocking chair while I changed into my pajamas and crawled into bed. She snuggled in with me and was soon fast asleep. Not so for me. I spent a fitful night, waking often to make sure she was still breathing.

The next day we took the little white dog to MSU ER veterinary hospital and after several days and many tests—including an echocardio-gram and two CT scans—we learned that Sally had three tumors. One inoperable tumor was on her heart and partially blocking not one, but two, pulmonary arteries. Leave it to Sally to go to the extreme.

We had numerous discussions with Dr. San-toro Beer, Sally's treating MSU doctor (and our son-in-law's cousin), an MSU surgeon, and Dr. Moore about options for Sally. These included surgeries and/or radiation—which would be five days a week for six weeks. Mike and I then did a lot of talking and crying, and more talking and more crying. What would be best for our 11-year-old little furry girl?

After a great deal of love-searching, we decid-ed we would forego any additional medical treatment and make the remainder of our time with Sally the best it could be.

Sally helped with this decision in that she has had no more passing out episodes and seems to be fine—great, actually. She is playing with Eli, spinning with happiness, annoying Socks (our 18-year-old cat), and snuggling as much as possible. She is even—are you ready for this?—eating out of a bowl. Seriously! Of course, we have upped the taste factor by adding canned food, but we didn't expect that change. I guess miracles do happen.

There is no way of knowing how much longer Sally will grace us with her presence, but I will take any amount of time and she will love, and be loved, every minute. It could be weeks, months or even years—we just don't know. What we do know is that she will be spoiled even more than she already has been (is that possible?), and I will always have my lap ready for snuggling.

Thank you to everyone who offered comments on Facebook, sent cards, called or reached out to us. It was a loving reminder that we are not alone during this difficult time. A special thanks to the staff at MSU ER, Dr. Kari Santoro Beer, and Dr. Matthew W. Beal. Thank you also to everyone at Harborfront Hospital for Animals, Dr. Jim Moore and Dr. Joy Jackson. You have all gone above and beyond and we embrace you as our friends.

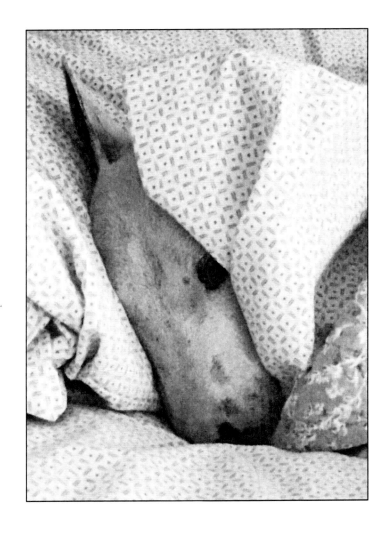

Rug Burn in a Most Unlikely Location

"Sally's butt looks weird," I said.

"What?" Mike asked. "Weird, how?"

"I don't know, just different than it normally does." Her butt was bright red and swollen. It looked similar to one of those ugly baboon butts.

Mike walked away shaking his head at my description, but I was sure there was something not quite right.

Later that day I saw Sally chasing her tail for the umpteenth time and I figured it out. She wasn't chasing her tail in the normal spinning around way—like most dogs—no, she was sitting on the floor while chasing her tail. That's right; she was spinning around on her butt and grabbing at her tail at the same time. She caught it occasionally too, which I thought showed real talent. It also explained the weird butt look.

"I'm pretty sure Sally has a rug burn on her butt, Mike," I said.

"Leave it to Sally to rug burn her butt," he said. "How many other dogs do you know that have rug-burned their butts?"

"The bigger question is how many other dogs chase their tail while sitting on their bums?"

The next day we had an appointment with Sally's vet to address her sleeping—or rather not sleeping—issues. She was waking up every night and staying awake for 3-4 hours. During those hours she would pace, lay down, get up, move to another spot, lay down, get up, and so on. Since she wasn't getting any good sleep, she was dragging during the day—and that meant I was dragging, too. We needed help.

After Sally's examination and my discussion with Dr. Moore, we decided to try Xanax (for Sally, not me) and see if that would help her relax at night and stay asleep. I was more than willing to give it a try.

During the examination, Dr. Moore lifted Sally's tail to take her temperature. "That doesn't look good," he said.

"Right?" I then explained how she had been chasing her tail while sitting and the rug burn butt theory. I think I saw him start to raise his eyebrow at the spinning on her butt story, but anything with Sally was probable.

He gave me directions on how to gently wash her bum, pat it dry, and then apply some medicated powder on it. "Do this several times a day," he said.

That night I asked Mike to help me with the whole butt washing, drying and powdering routine. He held her and the whole process took less than five minutes. Sally didn't seem to mind at all. Later when she started spinning, we simultaneously yelled at her to stop.

The next day I was home alone with Sally when it was time for the bum cleaning. Since I didn't have anyone to help, I knew I had to improvise. I had her stand backwards between my legs. I then picked her back end off the floor and held her by pressing my knees together. I was then free to use both hands to scrub—ever so gently—dry and powder. It reminded me of when my children were babies and they had diaper rash. Except I wasn't holding them upside down between my knees.

A couple days later Sally and I were pros at this odd little endeavor. When I got out the medication, she would walk over and stand between my legs. Her butt was not as red and swollen, and the rug burns had scabbed over.

The Xanax was working too, and Sally (and I) was getting plenty of much needed sleep at night. This meant she was happy and playful during the day. Just what we both needed.

We're figuring things out as we journey down this new chapter in Sally's life, but I have to admit I never thought I was ever going to be powdering a little white dog's butt.

PS – No dog was hurt in the taking of this photograph, even though it looks like she is being tortured.

What Do You Want?

"Sally, do you need to go outside?" I ask, using my happy voice. "Good girl!"

I always sound extra happy when I praise either of the dogs for letting me know they need to go outside. Especially Eli because he often forgets he should go outside when he has to pee.

Sally and I have been in my home office for the past several hours. While I work at my desk, she snoozes and snores on her pillow. Every time I get up, I tell her to "stay" because otherwise she'll pop up and follow me. Often times I am only going to the bathroom and it makes me wonder what it would feel like if Sally barked at me with praise whenever I got up to use the bathroom.

Now I head to the back door with Sally trotting behind me. "You're such a good girl," I continue in my sing song voice. She and I step outside and I breathe in the fresh 54° March air. It feels so good to not be shivering in below freezing temperatures and telling Sally to hurry so we can run back inside.

Sally dilly dallies a little, but after a few minutes we head back to my office. I sit in my chair and turn to face the computer. Sally walks toward her pillow, but within minutes she is back at my chair barking.

"What do you want, Sal?" I ask. She looks at me with her deep brown eyes that are just starting to cloud a bit with cataracts. I bend down and give her long nose a few kisses and rub her head, then turn back to my desk.

She barks again, so I decide to ignore her and see if that sends her back to her pillow. She barks. Well, that isn't working.

"I'm not sure what you want, baby girl." It is too early for suppies and she was just out taking care of her business.

I walk to the treat jar on the bookshelf. She follows me and sits while I reach in and take out a doggy snack. Breaking it in half, I give it to her and she takes it gently between her lips. She munches it down, sprinkling crumbs on the floor, then looks up for the other half. I had intended to save that for later, but she knows I have a hard time resisting her Sally charm, so I give it to her.

I step past her and return to my chair and become engrossed in the manuscript I am working on, jumping when Sally barks at me again. She is standing behind my chair, tail wagging and staring at me.

"Seriously Sally, I have no idea what you want." I point to her pillow. "Be a good girl and go lay down."

Her head follows the direction of my hand and she looks at her pillow, then back at me. She barks again and again and again.

"What? What? What?" I ask. "What do you want?"

I stand and she heads for the office door. Stopping, she looks back as if I should be following her. Okay, I'll give it a try. She trots to the den and we walk into the room. Sally leads the way until she gets to the couch. There she stops and looks back at me. Her tail wagging so much her whole back end is wiggling.

"I still don't know what you want, Sally." A light bulb turns on in my head and I realize what she wants—a lap. And not just any lap will do. She wants my lap.

Sally has led me to the couch so I will sit and she can cuddle on my lap. *Seriously Sal?* I think. *I have work to do.*

I arrange a blanket in the corner of the couch and Sally jumps up. I get her snuggled in and head back toward my office. "Stay," I say as I point at her. "Stay." She hangs her head, but stays put.

In my office, I grab my laptop and glass of water before I head back to the den. I might as well get some work done while I'm sitting on the couch.

A Fork in Our Plans

A couple months ago we started mixing wet dog food with Eli and Sally's dry food. To say they were ecstatic is an understatement. You would think they had never eaten anything outside of dry dog food and that wasn't true. I am a terrible dog parent when it comes to people-food treats and Eli is self-recycling (I'll let you figure that one out for yourself).

So when we put the bowl—yes, the bowl—down in front of Sally we expected to get the look. Instead, she didn't hesitate to dig right in. She even licked the bowl—yes, the bowl—clean. Now, if you know Sally, you understand that she does not eat out of a bowl. Oh contraire. She eats her food off a mat in the shape of a dog bone. If you put a bowl of food in front of her, she will bark at it until someone (me) pours the contents onto said mat. So when she ate the wet/dry food

mix out of a bowl, Mike and I had a small celebration. Actually, at first we were confused and
then we high-fived each other. Sally was eating
out of a bowl—like a normal dog!

We were wary, but every day she continued to
eat out of her bowl. It was one of our cereal
bowls, but we were so happy to see her eating
out of something other than off the mat, we
would have fed her on fine china—if we had any.

Days went by, weeks went by and we were so
happy with our normal Sally. We relaxed into
this new routine and almost forgot about our
sweet little girl's propensity for oddness. Until
the day I heard her barking after I fed her. I was
concerned as I headed toward her with quick
steps and then it dawned on me. "Noooo," I said
in despair. My steps slowed and sure enough,
there was Sally facing her half-full bowl of
wet/dry food and barking at it.

"Come on, Sally," I said, shaking the bowl a
little. "You can do it. You can be a normal dog."

She gave me her 'are you crazy' look and
barked again. "Sally, I am not pouring this food
onto the mat," I said with the sternness in my
voice she always ignores. "I know you can eat out
of the bowl." I turned, walked out of the room
and hid behind door.

When I heard the food move in the dish I said
a silent "yes" as I peeked around the corner. She
was only pushing the bowl across the floor with

her nose. Arrggg! This was not the outcome I expected or wanted.

Admitting defeat, I grabbed a fork and scraped the leftovers onto her mat. She glanced up at me with a look of smugness (okay maybe I imagined that) and gobbled up the food. I took the fork and the bowl into the kitchen where Eli was waiting. He, of course, had eaten his food in record time and was now looking at the items in my hand with drooling expectation. I set them down and he licked them both clean.

This new feeding routine continued for months. It consisted of 1) filling Sally's bowl with food (with the hope that she would eat like a normal dog); 2) placing the bowl on the floor for her; 3) waiting for the inevitable bark after she ate a little; 4) scraping the leftovers onto said mat; and, 5) giving the fork and bowl to Eli for cleaning. We had once again been trained by Sally.

One evening after Mike got home from work, he was giving Eli his usual hugs. Eli was sitting on the recliner in the bedroom which was where he could be found most days.

Now Eli loves to take things and hoard them. Whenever he is in my office and takes off on a run, I find him on said chair with paper, a book or anything else he has had the opportunity to grab. Shoes are among his favorite items, especially guest's shoes. He has also taken eyeglasses, clothes, and blankets. Yes, even blankets.

"Tricia," Mike said. "Come look at this."

I was in the kitchen cleaning up, but stopped and went to the door.

"What?" I said.

"Come here." He motioned me to come to Eli's chair.

Lying next to Eli was the cleanest fork I have ever seen. He had obviously spent a great deal of time licking it after he swiped it. What his intent was for the fork, I'm not sure, I'm just glad we saw it before either of us sat on the chair with him.

A Saturday in the Life of Sally

The day started at 4:00 am when Sally's cold nose sniffed my eyelid. It was an interesting, if not terrifying way to be startled from sleep. I lifted the blanket, thinking she just wanted to snuggle, but instead she sat on my arm. Now I was fully awake and realized I had forgotten to give her the doggy Xanax she needs to sleep through the night. She (we) would not be going back to sleep without it, so we got up. After a trip outside to pee (her, not me), her meds, a trip to the bathroom (me, not her), we snuggled back into the blankets and slept for another four hours.

After breakfast, a few errands on my part, and another nap on hers, we all (Mike, Eli, Sally and I) headed outside. It was sunny, warming up, and there were flowers to be planted (my job), mulch to be spread (Mike's job), chipmunks to terrify (Eli's job), and a new paddle boat to obsess over (Sally's job). Wait! What? Yup! Sally found a new obsession.

We were given the paddle boat earlier in the week by our friends, Joe and Michelle. I was ecstatic as I had wanted to paddle around in our pond since we moved in. Mike was not as excited because he had been putting me off since we moved in. I wasn't worried because when I'm happy, Mike's happy and I was really happy. Sally was intrigued, but not that interested when the boat was placed on the grass near the dock. She had sniffed it, but then lost interest until Saturday morning.

She was doing her usual running and happy rolling (not the kind that involves a dead or disgusting thing), but stopped when she got close to the boat. She lowered her nose to the ground and followed it to the water craft. She started running around it, poking her nose into every crevice that met the ground, and trying to get underneath. Our guess was that a tiny (now terrified) mouse had run under it when the large white beast arrived. The obsession had begun. For the next three (yes, I said three) hours Sally did not leave the boat. She barked at it, searched every inch of it, and once in a while she sat and looked at it. She even got Eli involved, but he gave up after a few minutes. Sally didn't leave for 180 minutes (give or take a few minutes).

After that she also gave up on the mouse (who was probably long gone) and spent a bit of time exploring the newly mulched gardens, relaxing in the shade of a Maple tree, scratching her back by wiggling in the grass, and looking for toads to lick (lucky for the toads, she didn't find any). She did find a shovel Mike was using and dragged it back and forth across the yard. She would pause, drop it on the ground, then grab it and take off again.

I was planting annuals in the upper garden when she wandered up and found me. She expressed her desire to help by sitting on one of the newly planted flowers. As I continued my work, she followed me around, albeit her enthusiasm for the beautiful sunny day was waning and her steps were slower. At one point, I bent to kiss her head and noticed she had rubbed her nose raw on the boat in her quest for the mouse.

My energy was waning too, and getting up from my squatted position while planting was taking longer, but I was determined to take my boat out in the water that day. Mike and I pushed it into the water and I climbed aboard. Sally and Eli had zero desire to go with me, so I started pedaling. It was as much fun as I imagined and as I looked around, I saw Sally running around the pond following me. Of course I smiled—most things involving Sally make me smile. After a short spin, I headed back to the dock.

Our day of outside activities was done and we all went inside. Mike headed for the shower, Eli dropped onto the pillow in the living room, and Sally and I collapsed onto our chair. It wasn't long before the melody of doggy snoring filled the room, and I was lulled into a short nap.

The dogs sprang to life when they heard Mike filling their food bowls and I wandered to the shower. After a few minutes, Sally walked in, stood on the rug and stared at me for my entire shower. Seriously, it was unnerving—even if it was just Sally. She wanted me to sit somewhere so she could sleep in my lap.

As I snuggled into the blankets with her later that night, I ran through the events of the day and held her a little closer. My little 12-year-old, cancer riddled, partially deaf Sally had thoroughly enjoyed her day and right then, that was all that mattered.

Sally's Bucket List

I saw a commercial that showed a man doing a variety of things with his dog that was on the dog's bucket list. That got me thinking about what would be on Sally's bucket list. I made the list and then realized there was a problem—but it was a good problem.

Lick some toads.
Happens every time she finds one.
Get a puppuccino at Starbucks.
Made a complete mess in the backseat with all the whipped cream, but worth it.
Nap in mom's office.
Is happening as I write this.
Play with a shovel or rake again.
Last weekend.

Eat a chipmunk.

By accident when the silly thing jumped into her mouth. Seriously, I saw it happen.

Drink water from a Dixie cup.

She gets this just about every night.

Take a vacation with mom.

She is going on a writing retreat with me at the end of June.

Wrestle with Eli.

Ongoing.

Stretch out on the grass in the sunshine.

Every sunny day.

Drink from a waterfall.

We have a waterfall in our backyard, so this happens quite often.

Sit on Santa's lap.

Has happened on several occasions. She never seems to enjoy it.

Harass the cat.

In a loving way, it happens daily.

Go to the beach.

Right in our backyard—done.

Swim in a pond.

Happened by accident and she hated it. Doubt if it will ever happen again.

Watch dog movies.

Always falls asleep. Just like her mom.

Go to bed early and get up late.

Done and done.

Have a book written about me.

Three done and one in the works.

Meet with children at their schools.

Yup. Been there, done that. Sort of loved it.

Have special friends.

Many are on that list.

Sit on mom's lap while she is working.

Tried—doesn't work well.

Chase butterflies.

Didn't end well for the butterflies.

Have my own Facebook page.

Check out Life With Sally.

Ride in an airplane.

Did this with two cats.

Become a world famous painter.

We'll just stick with taking a doggy painting class.

Eat fresh fruit.

Strawberries right off the vine and blueberries off the bush—done.

Take a ride in a kayak.

Lasted less than five minutes.

Wear silly Halloween costumes.

Okay, I added that one. Sally is not a fan of costumes.

Have a fan base of fish.

Happens every time she walks along the edge of the pond. The bass follow her as if she is the pied piper of fish.

Lay in a hammock with mom.

Was perfect and we fell asleep.

Chase chipmunks and other small rodents.

She chases Eli while he chases the chipmunks.

Hide in mom's perennial garden.

She's not very good at hiding.

As you can see, most of the things on Sally's bucket list have already done and I'm struggling to think of more things to add.

Based on how great Sally has been acting lately, I believe we have plenty of time to fulfill more things on her bucket list. Can you help us? What would you add to Sally's bucket list? Please email me at triciawrite@gmail.com and give Sally and me some suggestions. Your idea(s) might just land on her list.

What Has Sally Given Me?

As many of you know from reading this monthly column or the Life With Sally books, I was not a dog person when we adopted Sally. She was supposed to be my husband's dog, but Sally had other plans. Almost from the moment I pulled her out of the kennel and held her pee-soaked body against me, we were best buds.

Twelve years later and I know the cancer in her body is going to take her from me long before I am ready to say good-bye. Not that I would ever be ready. The other day I started thinking about everything Sally has given me and realized it is a long list of big and small things.

Bed snuggler. I was ready to be a good doggy parent and teach Sally to sleep in her kennel from the first night. Per the books I had read, I put the kennel next to my bed, placed Sally inside and when she barked, I tapped on the top and told her no. Then she started whimpering and that did it. I scooped her out of the kennel and into bed with us. She has slept with me ever since and she is the best snuggler, either lying between my bent knees or up by my stomach where I can spoon her. Lately when I wake, her head is on the pillow and she is looking right at me when I open my eyes.

Source of laughter. Bull terriers are described as clowns and in Sally's case, that description is very accurate. She seems to love to make us laugh. Seeing her run toward or away from us with her jaunty way of walking brings a smile to my face. Add to that the way she licks toads, drags rakes (and shovels) around the yard, eats raspberries and blueberries off the bush, and steals strawberries from your hand as you pick them—it is hard not to be happy around her. I won't even mention the laughter that erupts when we dress her as a banana for Halloween. Of course, that does not make her happy.

Lap companion. Sally loves my lap. I cannot sit anywhere in the house without Sally either on my lap, or trying to get on my lap. It works (and I love it) when I am sitting on the couch, in the overstuffed reading chair, or on the outside furniture. It does not work when I am sitting at my desk. We (Sally and I) came to that conclusion after many tries. There have even been occasions when I don't want her on my lap when I am sitting—like in the bathroom—but she thinks she should always have access.

Job creator. When Sally came to live with us I was trying to build my writing business. It was slow going until Janet (from this magazine) asked if I wanted to write a monthly column about Sally for *Cats and Dogs*. I agreed and the project was the impetus for my first book, <u>Life With Sally – Little White Dog Tails</u>. A few years later <u>Life With Sally – Still Spinnin' Tails</u> was written, and then <u>Life With Sally – Waggin' More Tails</u>. I self-published all three books and the experience aided me in creating my business, Splattered Ink Press. We help writers in all aspects of writing and publishing. But for Sally, I would not have started writing the monthly column, the books, and eventually create my business.

Overcoming public speaking fear. One of the things I had to do once the Sally books were published was promote and sell them. I had to get in front of people and talk—which terrified me. I joined a Toastmasters group where I learned to overcome my speaking fears and learned leadership skills. Sally and I were then able to make many appearances at events and in schools—a favorite thing for both of us.

Family member. Growing up, our pets were always disposable. If we got a dog, we would have him until he did something wrong and then we would get rid of him. This happened with just about every pet I can remember. As an adult, I never understood the concept of having a senior pet. When I met my husband, Mike, his dog was almost 10 years old and my first thought was, why have a dog so old? I had to re-think the importance of a pet's place in the family. With Sally, I have enjoyed spending these 12 years with her and watching as she gets older. I also know my heart will ache when I lose her, but that too is part of what being a family member entails.

This list could go on and on, but what it shows me is that what I have given Sally—a home, food, companionship and love, will always pale with what she has given me.

Back for More Tests

I shut the book after reading the same para-
graph twice and still not retaining any of the
information. Leaning back against the cup-
boards, I closed my eyes and focused on my
breathing. In out—in out—in out. It helped for a
few minutes until I opened my eyes and looked
around the veterinarian exam room. Thirty
minutes ago Sally had been sitting on my lap.
Now she was with the cardiologist and his assistant, performing a new echo cardiogram. We
were back at the same place where six months
earlier we had received the news that our little
Sally had an inoperable tumor on her heart. We
had been given different options, but had turned
them all down—deciding that at 12 years old all
the options would be worse for Sally than the
tumor. So we took her home with the plan to
spend as much time with her as we had. Unfor-

tunately, we didn't know whether that would be a month, six months, or a year.

I tried to prepare for Sally leaving me by talking and writing about it, but it didn't stop my tears from falling onto her fur as I snuggled her at night. I became obsessed with everything she did; trying to figure out if it meant her health was becoming worse. I fretted over her limping or sleeping more than usual. I saw her as dying, rather than living.

A lingering cough had brought us back to MSU and a follow-up visit with her cardiologist. Soon we would know the results of the test and how it compared to the previous echocardiograms. I had talked myself into believing there were two possibilities: 1) there would be no change; or 2) there would be changes that showed the tumor was larger and impacting her lungs. I wanted no changes, but I felt the growing tumor was more likely.

The sound of the doorknob turning brought me out of my thoughts and I stood as Dr. Olivier entered the room. He made a comment about Sally being quite the dog and I forced myself to laugh. It was a sound that didn't seem appropriate for the news we were about to receive.

"At the time of the last tests," he said, "the right side of her heart was two times the size it should have been. And she had a leaking valve."

I looked at Mike as I didn't remember hearing this news before. It had only been about the tumor, not anything else about her heart. My hands started to shake and I clasped them together and put them in my lap.

"Now the right side of her heart is a normal size and the valve is no longer leaking," Dr. Olivier continued.

What? I thought.

"What about the tumor?" Mike asked.

Dr. Olivier told us the tumor did not seem to be any bigger, in fact it almost looked smaller although that could have been from the angle of this test.

"Why?" Mike asked.

Dr. Olivier continued and stated he wasn't sure what the reason for the change was, but we didn't care at that point. We were just happy with the results. The cough could have been from allergies, but it wasn't from the tumor affecting her lungs. We asked him additional questions and he spoke with us for a few more minutes before he left the room.

To say we were stunned would have been an understatement. We looked at each other.

"Did that really happen?" I asked. Mike nodded and I wrapped my arms around his neck, still reeling from the good news. I had been ready for one of two answers, yet we had received news I hadn't even considered.

When they brought Sally back to the room I couldn't stop kissing her beautiful nose. I picked her up so Mike and I could kiss her on each side of her face. She didn't seem to mind.

The rest of that day and into the evening, I worked hard to see Sally and her antics as a part of her living, since I had been looking at her as dying for the previous six months. When she limped I saw it as a sign of her advanced age, or how she was trying to work us. Which of course always worked as she was a master manipulator.

As Sally and I got into bed that night, she wiggled underneath the blankets and snuggled up against me. It wasn't long before I heard her familiar snoring and I fell asleep smiling.

I Just Want to Write

Walking outside, I paused and let the sun warm my face. This would be a great place for an hour of Sally writing. I gathered my laptop, cell phone, pen, and headed outside. On the way, I dropped my pen and kicked it to the porch so Eli would not eat it before I could pick it up.

I opened my computer and brought up a blank page. My phone chimed which meant I had a text message and I spent the next 15 minutes texting back and forth with Splattered Ink's illustrator. After that, I texted our client to bring her up to speed on the project.

Sally gave me her "I want to be on your lap" look, so I moved over and patted the cushion. She crouched to jump, backed down, crouched, backed down, crouched...

"Really Sally?" I placed my laptop on the table and bent to pick her up. She moved out of my reach. "Fine, stay there." I pretended to lean back and when she crouched forward again, I grabbed her by her front legs and pulled her up. Eli was sitting on a chair and I swear I saw him shaking his head in a pitying way.

"Don't judge, Eli," I said, as he wandered away.

Sally settled and once again, I picked up my computer. My phone chimed and I responded to another text, and then decided to check Face-book—I was doing a good job of avoiding writing. During that time Sally left my side and Eli took her spot.

"What is that smell?" I gagged and put my hand over my nose. It was a smell of death coming from Eli's face. He gave me a dirty look.

"Come here, Eli," I said, turning on the hose. He went the other way. "Eli, come here." I grabbed him by his collar and rinsed him where he had rolled in something dead. I shut the hose off and went back to my computer. Eli walked over and there was that smell again.

"Ugh." It was going to take more than just water to get rid of this horrible aroma. I doused him with doggy shampoo, scrubbed and rinsed him off.

"I'm not enjoying this any more than you are Eli," I said. He shook, spraying me with water. I had a feeling he did it on purpose.

I settled back onto the couch, opened the blank document page and wrote a couple sentences. Eli was now rubbing his face in the dirt, but at least there was nothing dead there. That is when I noticed Sally doing the 'head lean' which meant she was about to drop and roll.

"No, Sally!" I rushed over and sure enough, there was the dead thing. Rather, the remains of the dead thing. A blue jay had been a meal for something and all that remained were a few gizzards and feathers.

I disposed of the innards, and once again sat to write. Eli was lounging on a chair, Sally was lying beside me and all was calm. Until a firecracker exploded somewhere in the neighbor-hood. Eli leapt out of his chair, jumped onto my lap, and knocked my computer onto Sally. I grabbed it before it hit the ground, while trying to calm a quivering Eli with my other hand. The calming was not working as he continued to shake—any loud noises terrify our little buddy. It was obvious he wasn't going to relax, so I put him in the house. No sooner had I sat down, then he pushed the screen door open and jumped up beside me landing on top of Sally.

I walked back into the house and called him. He went inside and I shut the main door. Sally was sleeping so I thought I could get back to writing. I read over the two sentences I had written and through the door window, I could see

Eli chewing on something. Inside I went—this time recovering soggy, torn papers stolen from the wastebasket under my desk.

Eli then bounded up the stairs barking. I followed and saw the UPS truck driving away. As I opened the door, Eli took off down the driveway.

"Eli!" I ran after him, stepping on tiny pebbles that dug into my bare feet. Sitting in the driveway, I rubbed the bottom of my feet and Eli came over to see if I had something he could eat. I brushed the dirt off his still stinky face and gave him a kiss. He offered his own lick and I tried not to think of the dead thing.

We walked together to the porch where Sally was sleeping and my laptop sat closed on the table. Opening it, I saw the battery was dead (another dead thing). I would need to charge it before it could be used outside.

I took a seat in the middle of the couch (on the hump) and Eli jumped up beside me. He put his head on my lap and we started to doze off with only the tiniest scent of dead blue jay still in my nose.

You Will Do As I Say

BARK!

"Sally, stop."

BARK!

"Sally seriously. I need to get this done. Go lay down."

BARK!

I swiveled my chair away from my desk and faced her as she stood next to me. It was 10:00 pm and I was trying to finish a couple of things before I quit for the day. "Okay, that does it." I picked her up, carried her upstairs and deposited her on the couch next to Mike. "Just keep her up here," I said as I went back to my office.

Less than five minutes later, I heard her nails on the stairs.

"Sally no," I yelled. There was a pause in the clicking before it started up again and soon she was bounding into my office, tail wagging.

I ignored her and tried to focus on my computer screen.

BARK!

"Sally, what do you want?" She wagged her tail again as soon as I turned and looked at her. I knew what she wanted. After all, I created this little dog's maniac ways. She wanted to go to bed and that meant I should go to bed, too.

I recognized defeat and shut off the computer. Walking up the stairs, I called her. She stopped at the bottom of the stairs, put one paw on the step and started barking.

"What's wrong with her?" Mike asked.

"She doesn't want to walk up the stairs," I said as I headed back down to carry her up.

"When did she decide she wasn't going to walk up the stairs anymore?"

"Does it matter?" I set her down at the top of the stairs and she followed me to the bedroom.

We live in a bi-level house and my office is on the ground floor. I will often let Sally outside my office door and then we walk all the way around the house to the front door (which is up a level), just to avoid having to carry her up the stairs. Does that sound ridiculous? It is.

A week or so later, my friend Lori was visiting from Colorado. We were standing in the kitchen chatting. Strange alien noises were coming from the bedroom. I was so used to the sound that it barely registered.

"Is that Sally?" Lori asked. "Is she okay?"

"Oh yeah, she just wants someone to pick her up off the bed so she doesn't have to jump down."

Lori shook her head in a sympathetic manner—or maybe it was disgust. I grabbed Sally and put her on the floor. Once again, I recognized the agony of defeat. Mine.

Let's not even get started on the wood floors, which she now refuses to walk on. I find myself carrying her from carpet to rug to wherever the princess wants to go.

At first I convinced myself that her refusal to do certain things was because she was old and arthritic. She would look at me with those big brown sad eyes and I would pick her up. It was easier, I thought. Now I realize she was just grooming me to become her personal mode of transportation.

Outside isn't much better. I will be settled onto the big comfy chair on the deck and she will stand in front of me, bumping me with her nose. I will scooch over and pat the space beside me. "Come on up Sally." She will sit on the ground and bark at me until I bend down and pick her up. I grumble and complain, but she doesn't care. After all, she has achieved her goal.

Last night I realized how ridiculous it had become when I got ready for bed. First, I carried Sally up the stairs after she barked at me to go to bed. I let her outside and then had to carry her over the threshold of the doorway when she wanted to come back in. Apparently, it was just too high for her to jump over, even though she has done it a million times. I went into the bathroom to get ready for bed and she followed me. While I brushed my teeth, she sat and stared at me—waiting for the drink of water from the paper cup.

Next, I lifted her up and put her into the bed. She sat on my pillow until I held up the blanket so she could wiggle underneath. When I climbed in, she rolled on her side and stretched her paws into my back. I was taking up too much room.

As I shut off the light I questioned how Sally and I had gotten to that point of total submission—mine to her. That is when she rolled over and snuggled against my back. The girl definitely knows how to work me.

Selfie

How many of you have taken a selfie? You know. Where you turn the camera around and take a photo of your face—or your face and those faces around you. I have taken many selfies. Most of them have been with my daughter, Nicole. Those are probably my favorites because we're being goofy and having fun together. I've even taken some with Mike, my husband, although he is not a big fan of selfies. So those aren't as goofy.

I believe there is an art to taking a selfie, which his evident in some of my first attempts. Those are the ones where some part of my face, usually my nose, appears very large in the picture. And not like, "oh you have a large nose," but more like, "wow, your nose is frighteningly big." You also want to make sure you get your whole face in the frame of the photo, but not fill the whole frame with just your face. Again, frightening. So I'm not ashamed to say that I've done a bit of selfie practicing and then deleted those photos so they weren't shared accidentally or otherwise with anyone else.

One morning I was sitting on the deck relaxing in one of our red lounge chairs. I had it kicked back all the way and Sally was stretched out on my tummy. The sun was starting to peek over the house, there were a few ducks floating in the pond, and Eli was under the table. Even Socks (our 17-year-old cat) was lying in a pool of sunshine, warming his old bones.

I was trying to take some photos with my iPhone, which took some finagling since I had to work around the little white dog on my lap. I took photos of Eli, Socks, my book, the glass of water perspiring on the table, the flowers in the rail box, and even the inside of the umbrella we sat underneath. By then, I knew I was getting bored.

I even took a few selfies, but there was a whole nose issue going on that I couldn't seem to overcome. And then it hit me—something that had never been done before by anyone—probably for good reason, but I ignored that last though. It was time for a Sally selfie!

She was facing toward me so I held the phone in front of her to snap the picture. She turned her head. I moved the phone, she turned her head again. I followed her face with my hand and she licked the phone. Great! Now I had dog slobber on my phone screen. Ewww! I wiped it off on my bathrobe and decided I needed to rearrange Sally.

I pushed and pulled until I had her face looking away from me, which meant I had her back end facing me. Not a good situation if she has gas. And sometimes, Sally has really, really bad gas. I think it may be connected to licking toads, but I'm not sure. Anyway, I needed to remedy this situation by getting the Sally selfie taken fast.

I got the phone adjusted in my hand and reached down by her face to take the picture, but my hand wouldn't reach that far. I leaned forward, the chair tipped and Sally freaked out by digging her paws into my legs and scooting backwards. This meant her butt was now closer to my face and the situation was getting worse. However, my hand holding the phone could now get in front of her face. I was able to snap a few photos before she tried to lick the phone again.

She got fidgety, so I pushed on her side and she spun around so her face was now looking at me. I gave her a quick smooch on her long snout, which was very kissable, and she laid her chin on my chest. Within minutes, she was snoring so loud I could barely hear the ducks.

I took a quick look at the photos and saw that I was not the only one with the large nose dilemma—or maybe it was "like mother, like dog." I contemplated taking a few more, but remembered how that furry butt had been dangerously close to my face. So I decided there was a first time for everything and sometimes a last—and a Sally selfie might just fit in both of those categories.

The Tina-Demon

My sister, Joyce, and her dog, Tina, have been living with us. Tina is a white Maltese/shih Tzu mix with curly white fine fur who weighs about seven pounds, which is a third of Sally's weight. We gave her to Joyce for her birthday, and I babysat Tina often. She was a quiet little fur-ball running through the house. Sally became her protector and would sit beside the floor pillow watching Tina as she napped. Tina would chase Sally around the couch—actually Sally would stand still as Tina ran around and around, giving a cute little yap when she passed Sally. Adorable.

Three years later and Sally and Tina still play together, but Sally is done with the game long before Tina. In fact, everyone in the house (including Joyce) is done with Tina's games before

Tina. She has definitely become the Napoleon of the household, and she doesn't let you forget it.

Tina does not like it when any of the animals—Eli, Sally or Socks (the cat)—get any type of attention. If I pat Sally on the head, Tina runs up and starts barking, excuse me, yapping. The noise that comes out of her little mouth is a series of high-pitched yips strung together making you want to pull your hair out. It hits you like the sound of fingernails on a blackboard, and is followed by a human voice (from whomever happens to be in the room) yelling, "Tina!" Of course, that doesn't change anything, so it is then followed by someone getting up and going over to her and saying, "Tina!" Depending on her mood, she will either look up at the person with a "what?" look, or she will walk away, triumph on her smug little face.

She doesn't bother Eli too much, probably because of the side-mouth sneer and low growl he has shown her on more than one occasion. But she sure likes to focus on Sally.

When Sally gets ready to jump on the couch or the bed to lie beside me, Tina goes crazy with the yapping, and the humans go crazy with the "Tina!" When Sally walks from one room to the next, Tina follows her—again with the yapping. You would think this little thing would go hoarse, but sadly no.

Tina's favorite game is when Sally is coming inside. Everyone will be out for a potty break (all the animals, that is—unless Mike is with them, but that's a whole different story) and Tina will run into the house first, then turn and lie down just inside—facing the door. Sally will come running up the steps with her happy feet, but once she looks inside, she comes to a dead stop and looks at me in a desperate plea. That is my cue there is something lying in wait. That something is Tina who is giving her "who me?" cute look, but as soon as Sally lifts her paw over the threshold, Tina pounces with yapping and getting all up in Sally's face. I have seen Sally turn and walk away from the door, refusing to come inside because of the Tina-demon waiting to attack. Maybe attack is too strong of a word because she isn't vicious, just annoying. Well, Sally might think that is vicious.

Lately I have been maneuvering one of my feet to hold back the tiny white yapper so Sally can come inside and slip down the hallway, away from the not-so-welcome Tina committee. This comes at a risk as managing the door, Sally, and Tina with my foot in the air challenges my coordination limits.

The other member of our family getting the Tina-treatment is our cat, Socks. He is 17 years old and loves to sleep like a log. He also does a lot of things which annoy the heck out of Tina, like breathing. When Socks walks into the room, Tina is right there. If Socks jumps onto the couch or stretches to get you to pat him, you guessed it—Tina is on him, sometimes literally.

Yesterday I was sitting in the family room with Joyce watching TV and out of the corner of my eye I saw Tina take off on a dead run to the doorway. Socks was walking into the room, until Tina jumped on his head and he fell backwards.

"Tina!" I yelled. She turned, ran back to us and leapt onto Joyce's lap, giving me the evil eye. "Did you see that?" I asked Joyce. Socks walked toward us, shaking his head.

"They play together like that all the time," Joyce said.

I was going to tell her I was pretty sure Socks might have a different definition of play, but Socks was getting closer to me, which set off the Tina alarm and I couldn't hear anything but yapping.

Joyce and Tina are moving into an apartment at the end of the week, so I had a long talk with everyone last night and told them we all just needed to be patient. Eli yawned, Sally wagged her tail and Socks fell over in a yoga-cat pose waiting for me to scratch his belly. And although we're counting the days, I know once Tina is gone we're going to miss the cute little rascal. Right?

The Tina-Demon

Sleepy Sally

Nap. I think that is Sally's favorite word. Or maybe it is bedtime. One thing for sure, the little white dog loves to sleep. It doesn't matter what time of day or what she may be in the middle of doing, if I mention bed or nap, I have her full attention. She might even like sleeping more than eating—and she loves to eat. And in full disclosure, I love sleeping with little Sally. She is an amazing cuddler.

She pretty much knows when it is bedtime, even if I plan on staying up a little later than usual. If I am sitting on the couch watching TV and she isn't already on my lap, she'll stand beside me and bark. Not a continuous stream of barking, just one quick bark to get my attention. Once I look at her she heads toward the bedroom. If I don't follow, she comes back and barks again. At that point I have two choices according to the little white dog. I can either follow her to the bedroom and go to bed, or I can convince her to snuggle on the couch with me until I'm ready. If I'm working late in my office, she will stand under my desk by my feet. If I don't get the message, she lays on my feet. Sometimes she will fall asleep there and her snoring will be enough to get me moving toward bedtime. She has pretty impressive snoring capabilities.

Sally and I do have a bedtime routine. I have always thought it was designed by me, but in reality she has had more of an influence than I realize. I go in the bathroom to change into my pajamas, brush my teeth and do all the stuff you do before hopping into bed. Sally lays on her floor pillow in the bedroom waiting for me. Once she hears the water running while I brush my teeth, she walks to the door and—you guessed it—barks. She won't bump the door open with her nose—that would be too dog-like. She waits for me to open the door and then she wanders in, stands on the rug outside the shower, then turns and stares at me. She doesn't sit, she stands and waits for her bedtime drink of water. I dutifully fill a cup and hold it for her. She drinks, well it is more like slurps, until it is gone. She then walks out of the bathroom and over to the bed where the princess waits to be picked up. I oblige.

Once I am in bed I hold the blankets up and she walks down to my knees where she turns and comes back toward my head. She stops at my waist, plops down and sighs. It is a happy, now-I-get-to-sleep sigh. A sigh I look forward to hearing. I then fall asleep to her snoring. The night is not over at this point though.

At various times throughout the night, Sally likes to rearrange herself. This consists of getting up, walking out from underneath the blankets and standing on my pillow—or my head—or my hair. Once awake, I automatically hold up the blankets for her to go back underneath, which she does. The routine is then repeated, complete with the sigh. This happens several times during the night. Needless to say, I haven't had an uninterrupted night of sleep in a very long time. I am so used to this sleep/non-sleep routine, that even when I am away and not sleeping with Sally I wake several times. I might even hold the blankets up in my sleep.

There is such a comfort of Sally sleeping against me and feeling her breathing. When we learned of her cancer and didn't know how long she was going to be with us, I would wake and put my hand on her—just to make sure she was still breathing. I continue to do this on occasion, even though her health has gotten better. The sound and feel of her breath going in and out is very soothing.

Some nights she will decide not to sleep underneath the blankets and her sleeping choices get a little interesting. I have woken to a black nose breathing on my face, which is better than a seeing a tail too close. Sometimes she will be sleeping along my back and decide she needs more room. She lets me know this by pushing all four paws into my back so I will move, which of course I do. There have been times when I wake on the edge of the bed, and it is a king size bed!

Oftentimes I wake with Sally's head on my pillow. When I open my eyes the first thing I see is her looking at me. I think about how much this little dog changed my life and how much I love her. I then wonder what she might be thinking. Maybe it is love she is feeling as she looks into my eyes, but more likely she has been waiting for me to wake and fix her breakfast. I'm happy with that for as long as I can.

What Do I Choose?

Last year was a tough year for our little white dog. It started out with her fainting four times in the period of less than 12 hours. That necessitated a trip to the emergency clinic in Grand Rapids, followed by a visit to the emergency room at MSU. Sally stayed overnight at MSU which was the first time I slept in my bed without her in the 12 years she has been with us. To say it was a long, fitful night would be an understatement.

We had to make some hard decisions once we discovered she had cancer with three tumors in her little body. Her heart was enlarged and there wasn't a specific reason for it. Plus, this cancer was not a type they normally see which was not surprising since we are talking about Miss Sally. This meant they couldn't tell us how fast the tumors would grow, or how long she would be with us.

The options included surgery and/or radiation, which came with risks and possible benefits. We spent many days in tears, talking it over with each other and friends. What would be the best thing to do for our little Sally? Radiation meant going to Lansing every day for weeks and that alone would be stressful for her, not to mention the actual radiation. Our decision was to allow Sally to live out whatever life she had left peacefully and without medical intervention.

I started waiting for her to die. Sounds awful, doesn't it? Everything she did was a concern to me. I sat up with her when she couldn't sleep, wondering if she was going to die in my arms. Whenever she was asleep, I stared at her to make sure she was breathing. I cried often. In my head I made plans for what we would do after her death. It was stressful, depressing and consuming.

Everything she did caused me concern. Walking instead of running. Drinking a lot of water, not drinking much water. Sleeping too much, not sleeping. It all pointed to her death and I was already grieving.

Months later she started coughing. This, I thought, was going to be bad. My imagination went wild with reasons why she would be coughing and they were all fatal. We took the long ride back to MSU so they could do a follow-up echo-cardiogram. We would then be able to see how her cancer was progressing. It was a quiet ride.

The cardiologist's meeting had a profound effect on me, not just in relation to Sally, but in how I was living my life.

He told us he had double-checked her last echo when he compared it to the one from that day as he couldn't believe the difference. Her heart was back to normal size and they couldn't explain the change. I had anticipated a number of different reports that day and none of them included good news. This wasn't good news, this was GREAT news! In addition, her tumors had not changed in size. The good news continued.

After the doctor and his assistant left the room, Mike and I stared at each other in disbelief. I scooped Sally into my arms and started kissing her long white nose. I couldn't contain my happiness.

"I wasn't expecting that news," he said as he scratched Sally's ear.

"I didn't either, but I'll take it."

We drove home smiling and chatting the whole way. Sally was in the backseat snoozing and I kept peeking at her. This time it wasn't with concern though, it was with joy.

At home, we took Sally and Eli for a walk around the pond and she was bounding along— just like usual and it hit me. She wasn't acting any different than she had before we got the new report. I was just seeing her in a new way. I was seeing her as living, not dying. It was an epiphany that I needed and it made me wonder how many times we do this with people who are ill. Do we see them as dying or living? How should we see them?

Since that day Sally has had additional small medical issues and our vet's office will always be on speed dial. I know her cancer will probably cause her death one day, but in the meantime, however long that will be, I choose to see her as living.

About the Author

Tricia L. McDonald is no stranger to writing. As owner and operator of Splattered Ink Press (www.splatteredinkpress.com), Tricia has a hands-on approach to guiding others in the writing process.

As a writing coach, Tricia works one-on-one with writers to hone their writing skills, edits manuscripts, facilitates writing groups, and helps writers prepare their manuscripts for publication. As a publisher, Tricia completes the process by publishing books both in print and eBooks.

She is an internationally published author, a public speaker and writing coach who lives and writes in West Michigan. On a volunteer basis, Tricia teaches writing classes to senior citizens.

Her Life With Sally series: Little White Dog Tails, Still Spinnin' Tails and Waggin' More Tails are compilations of stories chronicling life with her miniature bull terrier, and were published in 2009, 2011 and 2013 respectively. She also writes a monthly column, Life With Sally, for *Cats and Dogs Magazine.*

Tricia's book Quit Whining Start Writing: A Novelist's Guide to Writing (Mar 2012), is a guide to help writers put away the excuses and get the writing done.

Tricia has also been published in *Cup of Comfort for Mothers & Sons Anthology, The Breastfeeding Diaries Anthology, Mom Writer's Literary Magazine, Cup of Comfort for Mothers, I Love Cats Magazine* and *Oxygen Magazine.*

Life With Sally –

Little White Dog Tails, Vol 1
Still Spinnin' Tails, Vol 2
Waggin' More Tails, Vol 3

Available at
splatteredinkpress.com
and amazon.com.

$13.95 each

*Your copy will be
autographed by Sally.*